More Lundy Cookery

by

Ilene Sterns

Corydora Press

Copyright © 2021 by Ilene Sterns

The rights of Ilene Sterns to be identified as the author of this work have been asserted by her in accordance with the Copyright Designs and Patents Act 1988.

All rights reserved. This book or any portion thereof may not be reproduced or used in any manner whatsoever without the express written permission of the publisher except for the use of brief quotations in a book review or scholarly journal.

First Edition: November 2021

ISBN: 978-0-9566532-4-6

Cover photo and design: Ilene Sterns

Corydora Press, St Leonard's Cottage, Upper Minety, Malmesbury SN16 9P

www.corydora.co.uk

Table of Contents

Introduction	5
Shopping and Cooking on Lundy	6
Waste Not	8
Quantities and Measurements	10
Vegetarian, Vegan and Gluten-free Diets	11
Soups	12
Salads	22
Lamb, Pork and Beef	32
Chicken	46
Fish and Seafood	54
Pasta and Rice	64
Vegetarian Mains	74
Light Bites	84
Side Dishes	90
Baking	100
Desserts	108
More Salmagundi	115

Introduction

In 2020, the first edition of *Lundy Cookery* celebrated its 10th birthday. Since its publication, Lundy (like all of us) has changed. Toasters are now standard in the self-catering kitchens, and visitors will find a wide range of Free From and vegan ingredients in the Shop. As a result, the original *Lundy Cookery* had begun to feel rather outdated. So this year I decided to celebrate my favourite small island by creating an entirely new book: *More Lundy Cookery*.

During a recent trip to Lundy, I asked visitors as well as islanders what they'd like to see in the new book. I had lots of requests for vegetarian and vegan recipes, and people also asked for quick and easy dishes with plenty of flavour. You will find all of those things in *More Lundy Cookery*, which has been designed to make the most of the wide range of ingredients in the Lundy Shop.

Even though some aspects of Lundy have changed during the past decade, the island has not lost any of its magic. It is still the most restful and beautiful place I know, and I never tire of its unique character. I hope that this book will help make your home-cooked meals on Lundy as special as the island itself.

Shopping and Cooking on Lundy

Even though Lundy's self-catering kitchens are very well equipped, they do not have kitchen scales. So how can you bake a cake? Simple – you use either a Tala Cook's Measure or a Pyrex Kitchen Lab. One of these measuring jugs can be found in every Lundy kitchen. They have been cleverly calibrated to 'weigh' dry ingredients and they couldn't be easier to use. If your recipe calls for 200g of flour, just pour it into the measuring jug up to the 200g Flour line and then shake the jug lightly to level it off.

Even though the Tala Cook's Measure and the Kitchen Lab can both be used for measuring liquids, I would suggest that you use a traditional Pyrex measuring jug instead. The classic Pyrex jugs are made from heavy, heat-resistant glass and they have strong handles. Tala Cook's Measures are not water tight, and the Pyrex Kitchen Labs do not have a handle, so they are at their best when used as dry measures.

All of the recipes in this book were written with the Lundy Shop in mind. The Shop is small but mighty, and it stocks an impressive variety of products. It is also a sustainable business, which means that some items (e.g., fresh berries) are only available seasonally. By keeping plastic packaging to a minimum and working with local producers whenever possible, the Shop is able to reduce its carbon footprint while also benefitting the regional economy.

Even though the Shop now stocks gluten-free bread and biscuits (as well as lots of other Free From items), if you have specific dietary requirements it is always best to contact the Shop a minimum of two weeks before arrival to make sure you will have everything you need.

In fact, anyone can place a special order for food (of any kind) before they arrive on the island. If you know you will need fresh basil or a jar of tahini, for example, just order it from the Shop before your stay. After you have arrived on the island, your order will be delivered to your accommodation along with your luggage.

The Shop also offers an 'Order and Collect' service, which makes food shopping even easier. Just leave your list on the clipboard in the covered area next to the Shop. Two hours later, your order will be ready to collect.

Waste Not

Most of us are conscientious about conserving resources and reducing waste. But on a small island like Lundy, the choices we make are even more important. No one wants to bin good food but that's often what happens at the end of a holiday.

So what can you do to avoid food waste? Well, first have a look at **More Salmagundi**, which I hope will inspire you to treat your leftovers as the valuable ingredients they are, rather than as unwanted scraps.

Because it is a small island, Lundy's natural resources are especially precious. The island's water supply can be restricted at times and its electricity is expensive to produce. So conserving resources on Lundy is absolutely essential, and that same approach makes equally good sense at home. To help you get started, here are a few simple tips for reducing your water and power consumption.

1. Don't run the water when washing vegetables or fruit. Fill your sink with a small amount of cold water and wash the least dirty items first (e.g., tomatoes), saving the dirtiest ones (e.g., potatoes) until last.

2. If you need to boil water for cooking (e.g., for pasta), use your kettle to heat the water rather than boiling it from cold on the hob.

3. The hob is more energy efficient than the oven so if it is possible to cook a dish on the stovetop, do that rather than using your oven.

4. Use your oven more efficiently by cooking more than one dish it. For example, if you are roasting chicken or fish, roast a tray of vegetables at the same time. Even if you don't need the vegetables for that day's meal, they will make a delicious pasta or salad for the next day. Or use the extra space in your oven to cook white or brown rice, which is even easier than boiling it on the hob. Simply put the rice into a large heat-proof casserole, add water to the level of the first joint of your thumb (rest your thumb on top of the rice when you measure it), salt to taste, cover and bake. If the rice is not completely cooked when your meal is ready, just turn off the oven and leave the rice to finish cooking as the oven cools down.

5. If you've got room in a hot oven, try roasting vegetables or fruits that you would normally cook in other ways. Green beans, asparagus, sprouts, cauliflower, courgettes and broccoli are all delicious roasted. Simply toss them with a small amount of olive oil, add salt to taste and roast until tender. Apples, pears, peaches, grapes and plums can all be baked and served either hot or cold. Roasting or baking caramelises natural sugars and intensifies flavours, turning everyday vegetables and fruits into special treats. Use your roasted vegetables and fruits in salads, soups, pastas, wraps and desserts.

Quantities and Measurements

If a recipe in *More Lundy Cookery* calls for an ingredient that is sold in a tin or pre-packed by weight, you can easily 'weigh' it without having to use kitchen scales. For example, if a recipe calls for 100g of butter or 200g of digestive biscuits, just estimate the amount you need based on the weight of the original packet.

With the exception of the **Baking** chapter, most of the recipes in this book are quite flexible. If a salad calls for three spring onions and you only have two, there is no need to buy a third. The dish will be fine without it. Baked goods, on the other hand, demand a certain amount of precision. Unless you are an experienced baker, it's always best to stick to the recipe as written.

A note about serving sizes: most of the recipes in *More Lundy Cookery* will serve four people. But they can all be doubled (or halved) except for the baking recipes, which may not work properly if their quantities are changed. If you do increase a recipe to serve eight people rather than four, the dish may take longer to cook. So be sure to check it for doneness before serving.

More Lundy Cookery uses standard abbreviations for quantities, e.g., Tbsp = tablespoon, tsp = teaspoon, ml = millilitre, g = gram.

Vegetarian, Vegan and Gluten-free Diets

If you are looking for plant-based recipes, don't limit yourself to the **Vegetarian** chapter. *More Lundy Cookery* contains many recipes that can easily be modified for vegetarians and vegans – just look for the **V** (Vegetarian) or **V+** (Vegan) signs throughout the book. With only a few substitutions, those recipes can be turned into delicious vegetarian and/or vegan dishes.

The Lundy Shop caters well for vegans. It stocks a wide variety of products such as pesto and vegetable bouillon, as well as chilled and frozen foods. But stock levels do vary based on availability and demand, so if you require specific vegan items you should order them in advance of your stay.

In this book, recipes that are gluten-free are marked **GF**. The Shop offers a full range of gluten-free products, from baking powder to pasta, so anyone on a GF diet should be able to enjoy many of the recipes in this book simply by substituting one or two ingredients.

Soups

Soups are food for the soul. Comforting, easy to make and full of goodness, they are a great way to recycle leftovers. Almost anything can be turned into a tasty soup – I like to simmer leftover roast vegetables in a rich stock and then crush them with a potato masher. You can turn this thick soup into a hearty meal by adding crispy bacon bits or slices of cooked sausage.

For an easy cream of tomato soup, thin some passata with broth. Add a splash of cream and a spoonful of pesto and simmer to blend the flavours. Serve with garlic bread for a lovely light lunch.

If you've got fresh vegetables to use up, think minestrone. Sauté chopped onion in olive oil until soft, then add minced garlic and stir for one minute. At this point you can add any vegetables you've got handy –diced potatoes, celery, carrots and courgette are especially good. Stir in a tin of chopped tomatoes and some vegetable stock; cover, bring to the boil, reduce the heat and simmer for 15 minutes. Then add a tin of cooked beans and some small pasta shapes (raw or cooked). Simmer the soup for another 10 minutes or until the pasta is cooked. Top with grated cheese and serve piping hot.

The soups in this chapter are some of my favourites. I hope you will enjoy them as much as I do!

Bean and Pesto Soup

Serves 4: V, V+, GF

Bean and Pesto Soup uses only four store cupboard ingredients so it couldn't be simpler to make. But it is so richly flavoured and delicious that it tastes as if it cooked for hours. Turn this hearty soup into a warming meal by serving it with some crusty bread and a good cheese.

- Hot vegetable stock made with 800ml water and 2 vegetable stock cubes, crumbled
- 2x 400g tins cannellini beans
- 4 Tbsp tomato puree
- 5 Tbsp pesto

Rinse and drain the beans and put them in a large saucepan. Add 100ml of the hot vegetable stock to the beans. Using a potato masher, crush the beans to a thick paste. Don't worry about getting them completely smooth — this soup should be thick and a bit chunky.

Add the remainder of the stock to the crushed beans and stir well, so that the mixture is thoroughly blended. Bring the soup to the boil. Lower the heat, cover the pan and simmer for 10 minutes. Stir in the tomato puree and the pesto, then simmer the soup for 5 more minutes or until it is piping hot.

Lundy Miso Soup

Serves 2: V

Sue Waterfield, the manager of Lundy General Stores, has lived on Lundy since February 2015 and is the island's expert on everything Shop-related. She sent me this ingenious recipe for Lundy Miso Soup, which was passed to her by Charlie Smith, Lundy's heritage stonemason. Even though this soup does not contain any actual miso, it tastes just like the real thing.

- 1 Tbsp vegetable oil
- 1 red chilli, finely sliced (include the seeds if you prefer it extra spicy)
- 2 medium carrots, peeled and cut into 3mm batons
- 1 garlic clove, grated
- 1 Tbsp fresh ginger, grated
- Hot vegetable stock made with 1 litre water and 2 vegetable stock cubes, crumbled
- 1 Tbsp smooth peanut butter
- 3 Tbsp soy sauce
- 2 Tbsp sweet chilli sauce
- 1/2 bag fresh spinach
- 4 spring onions, cut into 2cm lengths
- Any other vegetables you might have in the fridge, cut into bite-sized pieces

- 1 nest of dried egg noodles
- 2 eggs, hardboiled and halved
- Cooked chicken (thin slices), frozen prawns (defrosted) or tofu cubes, if desired

Heat the oil in a small saucepan over medium heat and sauté the chilli for one minute. Add the garlic and ginger and stir fry until softened. Remove from the heat and set aside.

Pour the stock into a large saucepan. Over medium-high heat, whisk in the peanut butter until it is completely dispersed. Bring the stock up to a gentle boil and add the sautéed chilli, carrots, ginger and garlic. Stir the stock mixture and then add the soy sauce, sweet chilli sauce, spinach, spring onions and any other vegetables you might be using. Add the dried noodles and mix well. If you are using prawns, you can add them to the soup at this point. Simmer the mixture for 3-5 minutes, or until the noodles (and prawns) are thoroughly cooked.

Taste the soup and add more soy sauce, if you would like a richer flavour. Float the hardboiled egg halves carefully on top of the soup. If you are using chicken or tofu, add them at this point and simmer until everything is warmed through. Divide the soup between two bowls and serve immediately.

Caribbean-style Rice and Bean Soup

Serves 4: V, V+, GF

Coconut milk adds a lovely richness to this substantial main-course soup, and spinach adds a fresh note. If you like spicy food, feel free to add more chillies. This simple recipe can easily be altered to suit vegetarians or vegans.

- 2 Tbsp vegetable oil
- 100g bacon, chopped (if desired)
- 1 onion, finely chopped
- 2 garlic cloves, finely minced
- 1 fresh chilli, finely minced (or to taste)
- 250g (or 1 mug) of basmati rice, rinsed and drained
- 1 tsp dried thyme
- 400g tin red kidney beans, rinsed and drained
- Hot chicken or vegetable stock, made with 900ml water and 2 stock cubes
- 400g tin coconut milk
- 200g fresh spinach leaves, washed and shredded
- Salt and pepper, to taste

In a large saucepan, heat the oil and sauté the chopped bacon (if using). Drain excess fat, remove bacon to a plate. Add the onion, garlic and chilli to the hot oil and cook, stirring, for 5 minutes or until the onion has softened.

Add the rice to the vegetables and sauté, stirring, until the grains are translucent (1-2 minutes). Stir in the thyme, kidney beans and hot stock and mix well. Bring the mixture to the boil, reduce the heat and cover. Simmer for 30 minutes or until the rice is cooked.

Pour in the coconut milk and heat, stirring, for another 3 minutes. To finish, add the shredded spinach and continue to cook for 3-5 minutes or until the spinach has wilted. Season to taste and serve.

Corn Chowder

Serves 4: V, V+

Sweetcorn is the star of this old-fashioned chunky American soup, which can easily be modified for vegetarian or vegan diets. For a more substantial soup, add a tin of drained cannellini beans along with the sweetcorn.

- 4 rashers of bacon, finely chopped (or 2 Tbsp butter or vegetable oil)
- 1 small onion, finely chopped
- 1/2 green pepper, finely chopped
- 2 medium potatoes, peeled and chopped into small cubes
- Hot vegetable stock made with 500ml water and 1 vegetable stock cube, crumbled
- 3 Tbsp plain flour
- 500ml milk (or milk substitute)
- 1 tin sweetcorn (285g drained) or 2 mugs full of frozen sweetcorn, defrosted
- Salt and ground black pepper, to taste
- Paprika, to serve (if desired)

In a large saucepan, sauté the chopped bacon (or heat the butter or oil). Drain excess fat if using bacon. Add the onion and green pepper to the same pan and sauté until golden brown.

Add the potatoes, water and stock cube to the pan and bring the mixture to the boil. Cover and simmer over low heat for 20 minutes or until the potatoes are cooked.

In a small saucepan, combine the flour with 125ml of the milk (or milk substitute). Stirring constantly, bring this mixture to the boil. Pour it into the cooked potato and vegetable soup; stir well to combine. Cook the soup over medium heat for 5 minutes, then add the remainder of the milk and the sweetcorn. Continue to heat until piping hot but do not allow the soup to boil. Season with salt and plenty of black pepper. Serve sprinkled with paprika, if desired.

Cajun Fish Soup

Serves 4: GF

This hearty New Orleans-style soup can be as mild or as spicy as you'd like. Change it up by using prawns instead of fish. Cubes of cooked chicken, ham or sausage also make good additions. Serve with crusty bread for a quick and delicious meal.

- 1 Tbsp vegetable oil
- 1 onion, finely chopped
- 1 garlic clove, finely minced
- 1 celery stick, finely chopped
- 1 green pepper, finely chopped
- 1 tsp thyme or mixed herbs
- Chilli powder or Tabasco sauce (to taste)
- 400g tin chopped tomatoes
- Hot chicken stock made with 500ml water and 1 chicken stock cube, crumbled
- 80g rice
- 350g white fish fillets, defrosted and cut into bite-sized cubes
- 100g tinned sweetcorn, drained, or 1 teacup full of frozen sweetcorn
- Salt and pepper, to taste

Heat the oil in a large saucepan and add the onion, garlic, celery and green pepper. Sauté gently, stirring, for 5 minutes or until the vegetables have softened. Add the herbs, chilli powder, tomatoes and stock and bring the mixture to the boil.

Stir in the rice, reduce the heat, cover and simmer for 10 minutes. Add the fish and sweetcorn, along with any cooked meats you might be using, and return the soup to a gentle simmer. Cover and continue to simmer for another 5 minutes or until the rice is fully cooked and the fish flakes easily. Season to taste with salt and pepper and serve immediately.

Salads

Carrot Salad with Lemon Mustard Dressing

Serves 4: V, V+, GF

This lively and refreshing salad is great year round. It keeps well in the fridge and makes a colourful addition to a salad platter. Or try it stuffed into pitta bread, topped with hummus and fresh spinach leaves.

- Juice of 2 lemons
- 6 Tbsp olive oil
- 1 Tbsp wholegrain mustard
- 2 spring onions, finely minced
- Salt and pepper, to taste
- 4 large carrots, peeled and cut into julienne strips
- 700ml water
- 1 tsp sugar

Combine the lemon juice, olive oil, mustard, spring onions and seasonings in a jug and whisk until well blended.

Place the carrots, water, sugar and a pinch of salt into a large saucepan. Bring to the boil, lower the heat, cover and simmer until tender (test after 5 minutes).

Drain the carrots and run them under cold running water to prevent further cooking. Drain again and transfer to a bowl.

Add the well-mixed dressing to the carrots and toss lightly to coat. Season to taste. Chill until ready to serve.

Fattoush (Pitta Bread Salad)

Serves 4: V, V+

Fattoush is the perfect Lundy recipe. Created by frugal Middle Eastern cooks, it turns leftover pitta bread into a delicious and hearty salad. Get creative with Fattoush – it is a great way to use up the leftovers in your fridge!

- 2 pitta breads
- 4 tomatoes, diced
- 3 spring onions, chopped
- 6 radishes, chopped
- 1 red or green pepper, chopped
- 1/2 head iceberg lettuce, chopped
- 1/2 cucumber, chopped
- 125ml olive oil
- Juice of one lemon
- Salt and pepper, to taste
- 1 Tbsp mint sauce or pesto, if desired
- Optional ingredients: cooked chickpeas or lentils, grated carrots, chopped celery, olives, tinned tuna, raisins, chopped nuts, crumbled feta or blue cheese

Preheat the oven to 180 degrees. Place the pitta breads on a baking tray and bake until crisp, about 10 minutes. Allow the breads to cool, then break into rough 4cm pieces.

In a small bowl, whisk together the olive oil, lemon juice, salt and pepper and mint sauce or pesto (if using). In a large bowl, combine the torn pitta bread with all of the salad vegetables. Pour over the dressing and mix gently. Add any of the optional ingredients you'd like and toss again, to combine. Serve the salad immediately, so that the pitta does not get soggy.

Tunisian Cooked Vegetable Salad

Serves 4: V, V+, GF

Cooked vegetables are the stars of this spicy Middle Eastern salad. Tunisian Cooked Vegetable Salad keeps very well, and in fact, tastes even better after a day or two in the fridge. Any leftover salad can be tossed with hot pasta for an easy supper or stuffed into pitta bread and topped with some cooling tzatziki for a quick veggie sandwich.

- 3 Tbsp olive oil
- 1 onion, chopped
- 2 medium courgettes, sliced
- 1 large aubergine, cubed
- 2 garlic cloves, finely minced
- 2 red peppers, chopped
- 4 tomatoes, chopped
- 1-2 fresh chillies, finely minced (or to taste)
- Salt and pepper, to taste
- Feta cheese, crumbled, to serve (optional)

Heat the olive oil in a large pan and add the onion, courgettes, aubergine and garlic. Cook over medium heat for about 10 minutes, stirring occasionally.

Add the peppers, tomatoes and chillies (if using) along with salt and pepper to taste. Continue to cook over low heat, stirring occasionally, until the vegetables are tender and most of the liquid has evaporated (15-20 minutes).

Cool and chill the salad. Serve it cold or at room temperature, topped with crumbled feta cheese, if desired.

Sweet Potato Salad

Serves 2: V, V+, GF

This colourful salad is full of contrasting flavours and textures. Served warm or at room temperature, it makes a delicious vegan main but also works well as a side dish with pork or lamb.

- 2 large sweet potatoes, peeled and cut into 2cm cubes
- 2 Tbsp balsamic vinegar
- 2 Tbsp wholegrain mustard
- 60ml olive oil
- Salt and pepper, to taste
- 2 sticks celery, chopped
- 1 red pepper, chopped
- 1 spring onion, cut into 1cm lengths
- Lettuce or salad leaves, to serve
- Chopped nuts or feta cheese, crumbled (if desired)

Put the sweet potatoes into a medium saucepan and add enough water to cover. Bring to the boil, cover and simmer gently until potatoes are just tender (check after 7 minutes). Drain and set aside to cool.

While the potatoes are cooking, whisk the vinegar, mustard and olive oil in a small bowl. Add salt and pepper to taste.

In a large bowl, combine the slightly cooled potatoes with the celery, red pepper and spring onion. Add the dressing and toss gently to mix. Serve the salad warm (or allow it to cool to room temperature), on a bed of lettuce or salad leaves. For a more substantial meal, top with chopped nuts or crumbled feta cheese, if desired.

Cobb Salad

V, V+, GF

The legendary Cobb Salad is the 20th century Hollywood version of a Salmagundi. It was invented in 1937 at the famous Brown Derby Restaurant in Los Angeles, by a chef who recognised leftover ingredients as the secret to a great dish.

My recipe starts with a list of typical Cobb Salad ingredients, but don't feel that you have to stick to these suggestions — go ahead and use whatever you've got in the fridge, in any quantities. Your salad will be a Cobb Salad as long as all of the ingredients are finely chopped and mixed with the dressing just before serving.

By the way, the Cobb Salad's 3:1 vinaigrette dressing is a true classic, which keeps very well. If you love salads, make this dressing in quantity and store it in the fridge. Add any fresh or dried herbs you like, for extra flavour.

- Raw vegetables: tomatoes, spring onions, iceberg lettuce, radishes, red or green peppers, cucumber and/or avocado, all finely chopped
- Cooked vegetables, any variety, finely chopped
- Cooked beans (any variety)
- Cooked chicken, bacon or ham, finely chopped

- Hard boiled eggs, finely chopped
- Blue cheese, feta cheese or vegan cheese, finely chopped
- To garnish: toasted nuts or seeds of any kind
- *For the 3:1 vinaigrette dressing*:
- 1/2 tsp salt
- 1/2 tsp prepared mustard
- 2 Tbsp balsamic vinegar
- 6 Tbsp olive oil

First, make the dressing: place the salt, mustard, vinegar and oil in a small bowl and whisk until well mixed. This recipe can easily be extended if you would like more dressing — simply keep the 3:1 oil to vinegar ratio the same and add more seasonings as desired.

If you would like to present your beautifully arranged Cobb Salad at the table, the classic method is as follows: place the chopped lettuce in the bottom of a large bowl. Arrange each ingredient separately in long rows on top of the lettuce, so that the entire lettuce base is covered. Bring the salad to the table, pour over the dressing and toss thoroughly to mix. Garnish with nuts or seeds, if desired.

If you prefer your salad ready mixed, simply combine all of the ingredients in a large bowl and mix with the dressing. Garnish with nuts or seeds, if desired.

Lamb, Pork and Beef

Lamb and Sweet Potato Stew

Serves 4: GF

An easy one-pot meal, made even better if you can get tender Lundy lamb. This richly flavoured stew doesn't require much oversight and is even tastier the second day, so it is perfect for a make-ahead meal.

- 1 Tbsp vegetable oil
- 700g lamb for stew, defrosted and cut into 2cm chunks
- 1 large onion, finely chopped
- 2 cloves garlic, finely chopped
- 400g tinned tomatoes
- 1 tsp turmeric
- 1 tsp ground coriander
- 1/2 tsp chilli powder, or to taste
- 2 sweet potatoes, peeled and cubed
- 1 tea cup full of frozen peas
- Salt and pepper, to taste
- Greek yoghurt, to serve
- Mango chutney, if desired

Heat the oil in a large saucepan over medium-high heat.

Season the lamb with salt and pepper then brown it in batches, removing the browned meat to a plate. Reduce the heat to medium, add the onion and garlic to the pan and sauté until golden. Stir in the tomatoes, turmeric, coriander and chilli powder, breaking the tomatoes up with spoon. Return the browned lamb to the pan, cover and simmer until the lamb is just tender (about 30 minutes).

Add the sweet potatoes to the stew and simmer until the potatoes are tender, about 20 minutes more. Add the peas and simmer for an additional 5 minutes or until the peas are cooked. Season to taste with salt and pepper.

Ladle the stew into bowls. Top with a dollop of yoghurt to serve, along with a spoonful of mango chutney, if desired. Lamb and Sweet Potato Stew keeps well in the fridge, so it can be made a day ahead and reheated before serving.

Lamb and Lentil Ragout

Serves 4: GF

This hearty ragout is a great winter warmer. Easy to prepare, it will happily simmer away on the hob while you relax before dinner. Ladle it over freshly cooked small pasta shapes for a complete meal.

- 1 Tbsp vegetable oil
- 500g lamb for stew, defrosted and cut into 2cm chunks
- 1 large onion, finely chopped
- 1 large carrot, peeled and finely chopped
- 1.5l boiling water (or stock)
- 250g dried green lentils, washed and picked over
- 1 bay leaf
- 1/2 tsp mixed spice
- 1/2 tsp chilli powder (or to taste)
- Salt and pepper, to taste
- 2 large handfuls of fresh spinach, washed and shredded
- Juice of 1/2 lemon

Heat the oil is a large saucepan over medium-high heat. Season the lamb with salt and pepper then brown it in batches, removing the browned meat to a plate.

Reduce the heat to medium, add the onion and carrot and sauté for 3 minutes, stirring.

Add the lamb, water (or stock), lentils, bay leaf, mixed spice and chilli powder to the pan and stir well to mix. Bring to the boil, reduce heat and simmer gently for 1 hour, or until the lamb and lentils are both tender.

Stir in the spinach and lemon juice and cook for 1 minute longer. Season to taste with salt and pepper and serve over cooked pasta, if desired. This ragout keeps well and will taste even better after a day in the fridge.

Steak and Spinach with Mustard Sauce

Serves 2: GF

Even though Steak and Spinach with Mustard Sauce is the perfect special occasion dish, it couldn't be easier. But make sure you've got all of your ingredients ready to go before you start cooking — you will need to move quickly with this dish!

- 2 sirloin steaks, defrosted and patted dry with kitchen roll
- 2 Tbsp vegetable oil
- 30g butter
- 2 spring onions, minced
- 2 Tbsp brandy
- 1 tsp grainy mustard
- 1/2 tsp Worcestershire sauce
- Beef stock made with 60ml water and 1/4 beef stock cube, crumbled
- Fresh spinach leaves, to serve

Heat the oil and butter together in a frying pan until very hot. Add the steaks and sauté for 3-4 minutes, then turn them over and cook for an additional 3-4 minutes (you should see small droplets of juice on the surface of the meat when it is cooked).

Remove the steaks to a hot platter and keep them warm in a very low oven.

Reduce the heat and add the spring onions to the pan. Cook, stirring, for 3 minutes. Add the brandy, mustard and Worcestershire sauce and stir well to blend. Stir in the beef broth and cook rapidly to reduce the sauce by half.

To serve, arrange several spinach leaves on 2 serving plates. Slice each steak crosswise and arrange the slices on the spinach leaves. Pour the sauce over the steaks and serve immediately.

Chinese Beef Stew

Serves 4-6

A simple but flavourful slow-cooked recipe that works equally well with pork or chicken. Serve Chinese Beef Stew with fluffy white rice and your favourite green vegetable for an easy meal.

- 2 Tbsp vegetable oil
- 800g diced beef, defrosted
- 1 garlic clove, finely minced
- 2 spring onions, cut into 4cm lengths
- 2cm length fresh ginger, peeled and finely chopped
- 60ml soy sauce
- 2 tsp sugar
- 700ml hot water
- 4 carrots, peeled and cut into 1cm rounds
- 4 sticks of celery, cut into 2cm lengths
- Salt and ground black pepper, to taste

Heat the oil in a heavy large sauce pan. Working in batches, brown the beef on all sides, removing it from the pan and setting it aside as it browns. Add the garlic to the pan and sauté it for one minute (do not allow it to burn).

Return the beef to the pan and add the spring onions, ginger, soy sauce, sugar and hot water. Bring to the boil and skim off any foam that may form on the surface. Reduce the heat, cover the pan and simmer for one hour or until the meat is starting to become tender.

Add the carrots to the stew and simmer for another 15 minutes. Then add the celery and simmer for 15 minutes longer. Serve the stew on a bed of white rice, with the cooking juices spooned over.

Picadillo

Serves 4: GF

This classic Cuban dish couldn't be easier to make. Like all traditional dishes, it has many variations — some cooks add diced hard-boiled egg, crispy fried potatoes and/or capers for extra savoury goodness. Picadillo is usually served over white rice but you can also use it as the filling for Cuban-style pasties, which are perfect for a packed lunch.

- 1 Tbsp vegetable oil
- 400g minced beef
- 1 clove garlic, very finely chopped
- 1 large onion, chopped
- 12 green olives, pitted
- 1/2 teacup full of raisins, soaked in water until plump, then drained
- Salt and ground black pepper, to taste
- 250ml red wine
- 1 green pepper, seeded and chopped

Heat the oil in a large pan and brown the minced beef, breaking it up with a spoon as it browns. Drain off any excess fat.

Add the garlic, onion, raisins, salt, pepper and wine and bring to the boil. Reduce heat immediately and simmer for 15 minutes. Add the green pepper to the mixture and simmer for another 5 minutes (the pepper should remain crisp). Serve the Picadillo on a bed of white rice or chill it to use as a pasty filling.

Cheese-stuffed Pork Chops

Serves 4: GF

Pork and fruit are a winning combination and when you add cheese, you've got a dish that can't be beat. This versatile recipe can be made with any cheese, which makes it very handy for using up those last bits in the fridge. Serve the stuffed chops with mashed sweet potatoes and a green vegetable for a quick and satisfying meal.

- 4 pork chops, defrosted
- 50g Cheddar cheese, grated (for other cheeses, see Variations below)
- 1 Tbsp fruit chutney
- Salt and pepper, to taste
- 1 Tbsp vegetable oil

Cut a horizontal slit in each pork chop to form a pocket, taking care not to slice all the way through. Combine the cheese and chutney in a small bowl. Stuff one quarter of the cheese mixture into each chop. Press the chop closed so that the cheese doesn't ooze out during cooking. Season the chops, to taste.

Heat the oil in a frying pan over medium-high heat. Add the chops to the pan, lower the heat to medium and fry for 6-7 minutes. Turn the chops over and continue to fry for another 6-7 minutes or until the pork is golden and fully cooked. Serve immediately.

Variations: Wensleydale with Cranberries is perfect for this recipe. Simply slice the cheese, stuff it into the chops and fry. Camembert (or brie) mixed with finely chopped dried fruit is another good combination. If you'd prefer a savoury mixture, blend any blue cheese with a teaspoon of mustard.

Portuguese Pork Chops

Serves 4: GF

A friend gave me this recipe many years ago and it is still one of my favourite pork dishes. The tangy sauce is just gorgeous — try it with chicken if you fancy a change from pork. Serve Portuguese Pork Chops with cooked rice to soak up the delicious sauce.

- 4 pork chops, defrosted
- 2 onions, thinly sliced
- 250g fresh mushrooms, sliced
- 1 Tbsp sugar (soft brown is best but any type will do)
- 1 Tbsp tomato puree
- 1 Tbsp Worcestershire sauce
- 1 Tbsp vinegar
- Juice of one fresh lemon
- 1 tsp salt
- Pepper, to taste
- 1/2 tsp paprika
- 2 tsp grainy mustard
- 150ml water

Preheat the oven to 180 degrees. Spread the onions and mushrooms evenly in a roasting tin and arrange the chops on top of the vegetables.

Mix all of the other ingredients together and pour over the chops and vegetables. Bake for 45-60 minutes, turning the chops once during baking to ensure even cooking. Test the pork for doneness before serving (when it is fully cooked, you will not see any pink meat and the juices will run clear).

To serve, arrange the chops on plates and spoon over the vegetables and sauce. Serve with cooked rice, if desired.

Chicken

Apricot Barbecue Chicken

Serves 4: GF

If you love sticky-sweet barbecue sauce, this is the recipe for you! Serve Apricot Barbecue Chicken straight out of the oven for an easy meal. Or cook it in advance and enjoy it cold — it makes a great picnic dish.

- 1 Tbsp olive oil
- 2 garlic cloves, finely sliced
- 2x 400g tins chopped tomatoes, drained to remove excess liquid
- 75ml apricot jam
- 1 Tbsp balsamic vinegar
- 1 tsp salt
- 1/2 tsp pepper
- 4 chicken portions (legs and thighs work well), defrosted
- Additional salt and pepper, to taste

Heat the oil in a medium saucepan over medium-high heat, add the garlic and cook for one minute. Stir in the tomatoes, jam, vinegar, salt and pepper. Reduce heat and simmer until the sauce has thickened slightly, about 15 minutes.

While the sauce is cooking, preheat the oven to 180 degrees. Arrange the chicken portions in a roasting tin and season with salt and pepper, to taste. Pour the barbecue sauce over the chicken and cook for 50-60 minutes or until done, spooning the sauce over the chicken once during cooking. The chicken is cooked with the juices run clear when pricked with a fork. Serve the chicken hot, or cool it before storing it in the fridge.

Italian Chicken with Lemon and Wine

(Serves 4)

This quick, one-pan sauté is light, fresh and full of flavour. It is lovely served over white rice or it can be mixed into cooked pasta for a more substantial dish.

- 2 Tbsp olive oil
- 4 chicken breast fillets, defrosted and cut crosswise into 1cm strips
- Salt and pepper, to taste
- 2 Tbsp plain flour
- 1 medium onion, thinly sliced
- 250ml dry white wine
- 1 mug full of frozen peas
- Hot chicken stock made with 250ml water and 1 chicken stock cube, crumbled
- Juice of one lemon
- 4 Tbsp Grana Padano cheese, freshly grated

Season the chicken strips with salt and pepper and toss them with the flour. Heat 1 Tbsp of the olive oil in a large pan over medium-high heat.

Working in batches, lightly brown the chicken on all sides (1-2 minutes per side). Remove the browned chicken from the pan and set aside.

Reduce the heat to medium, add the remaining 1 Tbsp olive oil to the pan and add the sliced onion. Cook the onion until soft but not browned, about 4 minutes.

Return the chicken to the pan, add the peas and the wine and bring to the boil. Add the hot stock and stir well. Reduce the heat and simmer until the chicken is cooked and the liquid has reduced to a thick sauce (about 10 minutes).

Stir in the lemon juice and cook for one minute more. Taste the sauce for seasoning, adding more salt or lemon juice if needed. Spoon the chicken and peas over cooked rice, if desired. Sprinkle each serving with 1 Tbsp of grated cheese and serve immediately.

Braised Chicken with Leeks and Peas

Serves 4: GF

This simple braise will surprise you with its rich, savoury flavours. Even though the combination of ingredients may not sound very exciting, the end result is just gorgeous. Ladled over cooked rice and topped with a spoonful of Greek yoghurt, it is special enough to serve to guests.

- 2 Tbsp olive oil
- 4 chicken breasts, defrosted and cut into chunks
- 2 leeks, well washed and cut into very thin slices
- 150g smoked streaky bacon, defrosted and chopped
- Hot chicken stock made with 300ml water and 1 chicken stock cube, crumbled
- 2 tea cups full of frozen peas
- 1 Little Gem lettuce, halved lengthwise and finely shredded
- 1 tsp English mustard
- Salt and pepper, to taste
- Greek yoghurt, to serve (if desired)

Heat the olive oil in a large saucepan and brown the chicken breasts on all sides over medium-high heat (do this in batches so that the chicken browns rather than steams). Remove the chicken and set it aside.

In the same pan, sauté the bacon until brown and crisp. Pour off any excess fat, reduce the heat, then add the leeks to the pan and cook gently, stirring, until they have softened.

Return the chicken to the pan, add the hot stock and mix well. Bring the pan to the boil, reduce the heat, cover and simmer for 10 minutes. Add the peas and simmer for another 5 minutes, or until the chicken tests done.

Stir in the lettuce and the mustard, along with salt and pepper to taste. Cover the stew and continue to cook for 3-5 minutes or until the lettuce has wilted. Serve immediately, ladled over cooked rice and topped with a spoonful of yoghurt, if desired.

Soy Glazed Chicken with Roast Broccoli

Serves 4: GF

Make the most of a hot oven by roasting fresh broccoli alongside these tasty, soy glazed chicken portions. Accompanied by fluffy white rice, this East Asian-inspired dish makes an easy but elegant meal.

- 2 Tbsp soy sauce
- 2 Tbsp honey
- 2 garlic cloves, very finely minced
- 2cm length fresh ginger, peeled and very finely minced
- 4 chicken portions (legs and thighs are best), defrosted
- 1 bunch of spring onions, cut into 8cm lengths
- 1 head of broccoli, trimmed and cut into florets
- 2 Tbsp olive oil
- 1 tsp salt (or to taste)

Preheat the oven to 200 degrees. In a large bowl, combine the soy sauce, honey, garlic and ginger and mix well. Add the chicken and spring onions and toss to coat. Arrange chicken (skin side up) and the spring onions in a roasting tin. Roast on the upper shelf of the oven for 10 minutes.

In the meantime, toss the broccoli with the olive oil and salt. Arrange it in a single layer on a baking tray. After the chicken has roasted for 10 minutes, add the broccoli to the hot oven (on a lower shelf).

Continue roasting for another 35 minutes or until the broccoli is slightly browned on the edges and the chicken tests done (the juices will run clear). Serve with fluffy white rice, if desired.

Fish and Seafood

Orange Roasted Salmon

Serves 4: GF

Fresh orange adds a bright and zesty note to salmon fillets. The fish will 'cook' slightly as it marinates in the juice, which tenderises the fish and also adds flavour. Start this simple recipe about an hour before you plan to eat, so that the salmon has plenty of time to absorb the citrus marinade.

- 4 frozen salmon fillets, defrosted
- 2 Tbsp olive oil
- Juice and finely grated peel of one orange (grate the peel before juicing the orange)
- 2 cloves garlic, finely minced
- 1 tsp dried thyme
- Salt and pepper, to taste

Combine the olive oil, orange juice, orange zest, garlic, thyme, salt and pepper in a bowl large enough to hold the salmon fillets. Mix well. Add the salmon to the marinade and mix thoroughly. Marinate for one hour in the fridge, stirring gently once or twice to make sure the fillets are evenly coated by the liquid.

Preheat the oven to 200 degrees. Place the salmon skin side down in a lightly oiled roasting tin and pour the marinade over the fillets. Roast for 15-20 minutes or until just cooked through (the fish should flake easily when tested with a fork). Serve with cooked rice, if desired.

Feta-topped Mediterranean Fish Fillets

Serves 4: GF

Any white fish works well in this tasty, Greek-inspired recipe. Serve with rice or cous cous for an easy and delicious meal.

- 4 frozen white fish fillets, defrosted
- 2 tablespoons olive oil
- 2 cloves garlic, finely minced
- 1 medium onion, thinly sliced
- 1 green pepper, cut into thin strips
- 1 red pepper, cut into thin strips
- 2 medium tomatoes, cut into thin wedges
- 20 olives, halved
- Salt and pepper, to taste.
- 100g feta cheese, crumbled

Preheat the oven to 180 degrees. Heat the olive oil in a frying pan over medium-high heat. Add the onions and peppers to the pan and sauté for 5 minutes or until crisp-tender, stirring occasionally. Add the tomatoes, olives and garlic to the other vegetables and mix well. Season to taste.

Arrange the fish fillets in a lightly oiled roasting tin. Spoon the vegetable mixture evenly over the fish and top with the feta cheese. Roast the fish for 20-25 minutes or until the fillets flake easily with tested with a fork.

Seared Tuna with Pineapple Salsa

Serves 4: GF

Caribbean-style Pineapple Salsa will liven up almost any grilled meat or fish, and it also makes a fantastic dip for tortilla chips. You can make this dish as hot as you like – just add more chillies, to taste. Start preparing the salsa at least half an hour before you plan to eat so that the flavours have time to blend.

- 1 tin pineapple, drained and chopped
- 1 red pepper, finely chopped
- 1 chilli pepper, finely minced (or to taste)
- 3 spring onions, finely chopped
- 1 garlic clove, finely minced
- Juice of one lime
- Salt and pepper, to taste
- 4 frozen tuna steaks, defrosted
- 1 Tbsp vegetable oil

Put all of the ingredients except the tuna steaks and vegetable oil into a medium bowl and mix well. Cover the salsa mixture and leave it at room temperature for half an hour, so that the flavours can blend.

In a frying pan, heat the vegetable oil over high heat. Add the tuna steaks and sear them for 3 minutes on the first side, then flip them over and cook for another 3 minutes on the other side. As this point, the tuna will still be pink in the middle, which ensures it will be tender. Remove the tuna to heated plates and allow it to rest for a couple of minutes; the fish will continue to cook as it rests.

If you prefer your fish cooked through, leave it in the pan on low heat for another 2-3 minutes, checking regularly for doneness. Do not overcook, though, or the tuna will dry out and become tough.

Top the cooked tuna with Pineapple Salsa and serve. This dish goes well with cooked rice. Store any leftover salsa in the fridge.

Roast Fish with White Beans and Olives

Serves 4: GF

Simple to make but richly-flavoured, this one-dish meal relies on store cupboard staples. The fish is slow roasted at a low temperature for maximum tenderness. This same cooking technique also works well with salmon fillets, if you fancy a change from white fish.

- 1 tsp dried thyme
- 2x 400g tins cannellini beans, rinsed and drained
- 70g green olives, pitted
- 120ml white wine
- 4 frozen white fish fillets, defrosted
- Salt and pepper, to taste
- 2 garlic cloves, finely minced
- 1 fresh chilli, finely minced
- 1 lemon, very thinly sliced and seeded
- 5 Tbsp olive oil
- Lemon wedges, for serving (if desired)

Preheat the oven to 150 degrees. Mix together the thyme, beans, olives and white wine and pour everything into a roasting tin.

Arrange the fish fillets on top of the beans and season generously with salt and pepper, to taste.

Sprinkle the garlic and chillies over the fish and beans. Arrange the lemon slices, slightly overlapping, over the fish fillets. Drizzle the olive oil over the fish and beans. Roast for 25-30 minutes, or until the fish is opaque throughout and flakes easily when tested with a fork. Remove from the oven and allow to rest for a few minutes before serving. If desired, serve with lemon wedges for everyone to squeeze over their fish and beans.

Easy Creamy Prawns

Serves 4: GF

Even though this gorgeous dish takes only minutes to prepare, it is one of the most elegant mains I know. Serve the prawns over cooked rice or pasta so that you don't lose any of the rich, creamy sauce. A mixed green salad is the perfect complement to this sumptuous dish.

- 2 Tbsp butter
- 500g prawns, defrosted
- Salt and pepper, to taste
- 2 garlic cloves, finely minced
- 120ml double cream
- 25g Grana Padano cheese, grated
- Chopped fresh parsley, to serve (if desired)

Melt the butter in a frying pan over medium-high heat. Season the prawns to taste and add them to the pan. Cook, stirring, for about 4 minutes or until they are just pink and no longer translucent. Remove the prawns to a plate.

Reduce the heat to medium-low and add the garlic to the pan. Cook, stirring, for 1 minute or until the garlic begins to soften. Add the cream and bring up to a gentle simmer, stirring constantly. Blend the grated cheese into the sauce and continue to heat, stirring, until the cheese has completely melted (about 1 minute). Season the sauce to taste.

Return the prawns to the sauce and reheat very briefly. (Do not overcook or they will toughen up.) Serve immediately, garnished with chopped parsley, if desired.

Pasta and Rice

The Best Macaroni and Cheese

Serves 2-4: V

You may disagree with me about the title of this recipe, but please do give it a go — it is rich, creamy and delicious. The vegetables add a lovely green freshness to this dish, which needs nothing more than a salad to make it a complete meal.

- 200g uncooked pasta (any small shape)
- 300ml hot milk
- 2 slices of bread, torn into fresh breadcrumbs
- 225g Cheddar cheese, grated
- 1 small onion, finely chopped
- 1 green pepper, cored, seeded and finely chopped
- 3 spring onions, finely minced
- 1 tsp salt
- Pepper, to taste
- 2 eggs, well beaten

Cook the pasta until it is tender but still firm to the bite. Drain thoroughly and set aside to cool slightly.

Preheat the oven to 180 degrees. In a large bowl, mix the bread crumbs with the cheese and pour over the hot milk. Add the onion, green pepper, spring onion, salt and pepper. Stir in the eggs and then the cooled pasta.

Pour the mixture into a buttered (or oiled) casserole dish and bake for about 30 minutes, or until the macaroni and cheese is firm and golden-brown. Serve immediately.

Spaghetti Almost Carbonara

Serves 4

Spaghetti Almost Carbonara isn't at all authentic, but it is a real treat. Its Boursin-based cheese sauce is the perfect 'cheat' — use the same easy sauce to turn almost any pasta and vegetable/meat combination into an elegant and satisfying meal.

- 500g spaghetti
- 1 tea cup full of frozen peas
- 100g smoked streaky bacon, defrosted and chopped
- 6 spring onions, sliced into 1cm lengths
- 150g Boursin soft cheese with garlic and herbs
- 150ml milk (full fat is best)
- Salt and pepper, to taste
- Freshly grated Grana Padano cheese, to serve, if desired

Boil salted water in a large saucepan; add the spaghetti, return to the boil and cook for 7 minutes. Add the frozen peas to the boiling water (make sure it continues to boil) and cook for another 3 minutes, or until pasta tests done (you want it to be al dente).

While the pasta is cooking, sauté the bacon over medium heat for 4-5 minutes. Drain the excess fat, leaving 1 teaspoon in the pan. Add the spring onions and sauté gently for one minute longer, to soften.

Drain the spaghetti and peas and return to the same hot pan you used for cooking. Mix in the bacon and spring onions and set aside. Warm the milk in a small saucepan and add the Boursin. Mix the cheese into the milk, stirring constantly, to create a creamy cheese sauce. Heat the sauce until piping hot but do not allow it to boil.

Pour the cheese sauce over the spaghetti and other ingredients and toss gently to mix. Season to taste and serve immediately, sprinkled with grated Grana Padano cheese, if desired.

Pasta with Fresh Broccoli

Serves 2 (recipe can be doubled): V, V+, GF

This rustic pasta dish from Southern Italy is one to make when you don't feel like waiting for dinner — from start to finish, it takes only about 20 minutes. Don't skimp on the olive oil, which is the secret to this dish. Gluten-free pasta can be substituted if you are on a GF diet.

- 400g pasta shells (or another small shape)
- 1/2 head of broccoli, finely chopped
- 6 garlic cloves, finely minced
- 100ml olive oil
- Salt and pepper, to taste
- 70g Grana Padrano cheese, grated, if desired

Bring a large pot of water to the boil over high heat. Add the pasta and cook it according to packet directions until it is al dente.

While the pasta is cooking, heat the olive oil gently in a frying pan. Add the broccoli and garlic. Sauté the vegetables, stirring occasionally, until the garlic is golden (but not brown) and the broccoli is bright green and starting to become tender. Add salt and plenty of black pepper.

Carefully spoon some of the pasta cooking water into the frying pan and leave the broccoli to cook a few minutes longer.

When the pasta is al dente, drain it thoroughly and put it into 4 warmed serving dishes. Top each dish with one-quarter of the broccoli mixture and the grated cheese, if desired. Serve immediately.

Pasta with Aubergine and Mozzarella

Serves 4: V, GF

With its fresh-tasting tomato sauce and lots of lovely melted mozzarella, this dish is sure to please any pasta lover. Pair it with a simple green salad and some garlic bread for a gorgeous meat-free meal. Substitute gluten-free pasta for a GF diet.

- 4 Tbsp olive oil
- 1 garlic clove, finely minced
- 400g tin chopped tomatoes
- Salt and pepper, to taste
- 500g aubergine, cut into 2cm cubes
- 400g pasta (penne, fusilli or another small shape)
- 200g mozzarella cheese, diced
- 5 Tbsp grated Grana Padano cheese

Start by making the tomato sauce: heat 2 Tbsp of the oil in a small saucepan. Add the garlic and sauté for 1-2 minutes or until just softened. Add the tomatoes, season to taste and simmer over very low heat for 15 minutes.

While the sauce is cooking, heat the remaining 2 Tbsp oil in a frying pan. Add the cubed aubergine in batches, frying each batch until fully cooked. Set aside.

To cook the pasta, boil a large quantity of salted water in a large saucepan. Cook the pasta for 10 minutes or according to packet directions, until it is al dente.

Drain the pasta and return it to the large saucepan. Stir in the tomato sauce, the cooked aubergine, the mozzarella and the grated Grana Padano. Return the pan to the hob and cook over very low heat, stirring constantly, until the mozzarella is melted. Serve immediately.

Spanish Rice

Serves 4: V, V+, GF

Spanish Rice delivers all of the flavour and creaminess of a risotto without the stirring. It makes an excellent vegetarian or vegan main but also works well as a side dish with grilled meat or fish. Be creative with this dish — change it up with leftover bacon, ham, chicken or prawns, or stir in some chopped olives and top with grated cheese. Buen provecho!

- 4 Tbsp olive oil
- 2 onions, chopped
- 4 garlic cloves, finely chopped
- 1 tsp paprika
- 1 tsp turmeric
- Pinch of chilli powder, or to taste
- 350g Arborio rice
- Hot vegetable stock made with 900ml water and 2 stock cubes
- 500g vine tomatoes, chopped
- 2 Tbsp tomato paste
- Salt and pepper, to taste

- Leftover chopped bacon, ham, cooked chicken or prawns, if desired
- Chopped olives and/or grated cheese, if desired

Heat the oil over medium heat in a large saucepan. Add the onions, garlic, paprika, turmeric and chilli powder. Cook, stirring occasionally, for 5-10 minutes or until the onions are golden, making sure the spices do not burn. Add the rice and cook for 1 minute, stirring constantly, until the grains are translucent. Pour in the stock and mix well. Bring to the boil, reduce the heat, cover and simmer for 10 minutes.

Stir in the chopped tomatoes and tomato paste and continue to cook over low heat for 15 minutes or until the rice is tender and all of the liquid has been absorbed. If the rice starts to dry out before it is fully cooked, add a bit more hot stock or water to the pan.

If you are adding leftover meat or chopped olives, mix them into the cooked rice and warm through over a very low heat. Check the rice for seasoning; add salt and pepper to taste and grated cheese (if using). Serve immediately.

Vegetarian Mains

Three Sisters Stew

Serves 4: V, V+, GF

Native Americans often refer to the trinity of sweetcorn, beans and squash as the Three Sisters. Those crops were among the first plants domesticated by the ancient Mesoamericans, and they were always grown (and often cooked) together. Chillies and tomatoes also originated in Central America; in fact, our English word tomato comes from the Aztec 'tomatl'. Three Sisters Stew is a quick and delicious update of this traditional Mesoamerican dish.

- 2 Tbsp vegetable oil
- 1 onion, chopped
- 1 garlic clove, finely minced
- 1kg butternut squash, peeled and cut into 2cm cubes
- 400g tinned chopped tomatoes
- Hot vegetable stock made with 400ml water and 1 vegetable stock cube, crumbled
- 1/2 tsp paprika
- Chilli powder or Tabasco sauce, to taste
- 400g red kidney beans, rinsed and drained

- 285g tin sweetcorn, drained, or 2 tea cups full of frozen sweetcorn, defrosted
- Salt and ground black pepper, to taste

Heat the oil in a large saucepan. Add the onions, garlic, squash and a sprinkling of salt. Cook gently for 5-10 minutes or until the vegetables have softened.

Add the tomatoes, stock, paprika and chilli and stir well. Bring to the boil, reduce the heat and simmer, covered, over medium heat for 15 minutes or until the squash is tender.

Add the beans and sweetcorn to the stew, return to the boil and then lower the heat. Cover and simmer gently for another 5-10 minutes or until piping hot. Season to taste and serve with crusty bread for a complete meal.

Baked Corn Custard

Serves 4: V

Baked Corn Custard is American comfort food. In the US this dish would be called Corn Pudding, but it is not a dessert. It is an old-fashioned, savoury casserole which makes a delicious main course or a hearty side. Serve Baked Corn Custard with mashed sweet potatoes and cooked kale for a Southern-style vegetarian feast.

- 285g tin sweetcorn, drained, or 2 tea cups full of frozen sweetcorn, defrosted
- 1/2 tsp salt
- Pepper, to taste
- 3 eggs, lightly beaten
- 350ml milk (or milk substitute)
- 20g butter

Butter (or oil) a casserole dish and preheat the oven to 180 degrees. Put the sweetcorn, salt, pepper, eggs and milk into a medium-sized bowl and mix well. Pour the mixture into the prepared casserole and dot with the butter. Bake for 45 minutes or until a knife inserted in the centre comes out clean. Serve immediately.

Variations: Sauté 1/2 onion (finely chopped) and 1/2 red or green pepper (finely chopped) in a little oil until soft. Add the vegetables to the sweetcorn mixture before baking.

Baked Corn Custard is even more delicious with a topping of grated Cheddar. Grate enough cheese to cover the top of the casserole. After 35 minutes of cooking remove the casserole from the oven, spread the cheese evenly over the top and continue baking for another 10 minutes or until the cheese has melted and is starting to brown.

Spicy Coconut Cucumbers

Serves 2: V, V+, GF

If you've never had cooked cucumbers, you are in for a treat. In this quick vegetable sauté, the cucumbers are complemented by a spicy coconut sauce that would also work well with green beans or cooked squash. Turn up the heat by adding more chillies, if you'd like.

- 1 Tbsp vegetable oil
- 1 large cucumber, peeled, halved lengthwise and cut into 1/2 cm slices
- Salt and pepper, to taste
- 2 tomatoes, chopped
- 4 spring onions, thinly sliced
- 1 fresh chilli, finely minced (or to taste)
- 1 garlic clove, finely minced
- 150ml coconut milk
- 1 tsp honey (or sugar)
- Juice of 1/2 fresh lime
- Cooked rice, for serving, if desired

Heat the oil over medium heat in a large saucepan. Add the cucumbers and cook, stirring, for 2 minutes. Season to taste with salt and pepper.

Add the tomatoes, spring onions, chilli and garlic to the pan. Sauté until the vegetables have softened, 2-3 minutes. Add the coconut milk and honey (or sugar) to the mix and simmer until all of the vegetables are cooked through, about 3 more minutes. Add the lime juice and mix well.

Check the seasoning and add more salt and/or pepper, if needed. Serve immediately. This dish is especially nice when served over cooked rice.

North African Vegetable Stew

Serves 4: V, V+, GF

Exotic spices and dried fruits add warmth and richness to this easy vegetable stew. Serve it on a bed of couscous and top with feta and toasted nuts for a quick and satisfying meal.

- 2 Tbsp olive oil
- 1 large onion, thinly sliced
- 1/2 cabbage, thinly sliced
- Salt and pepper, to taste
- 1 large green pepper, cored, seeded and cut into thin strips
- 2 tsp ground coriander
- 1/2 tsp turmeric
- Pinch of chilli powder or a dash of Tabasco sauce, to taste
- 2x 400g tins chopped tomatoes
- 400g tin chickpeas, rinsed and drained
- A handful of raisins or sultanas
- Juice of 1/2 lemon
- Toasted almonds or other nuts, chopped, if desired
- Feta cheese, crumbled, if desired

Heat the olive oil in a large frying pan. Add the onions and sauté for 5 minutes or until soft. Add the cabbage, season to taste with salt and pepper and cook for 5 more minutes, stirring occasionally. Add the green pepper, coriander, turmeric and chilli and cook, stirring, for 1 minute.

Transfer the mixture to a large saucepan. Add the tomatoes, chickpeas and raisins (or sultanas) and bring to the boil. Reduce the heat, cover and simmer for 15 minutes or until the vegetables are tender. Stir in the lemon juice and check the seasoning; add salt and pepper, if needed.

Serve the stew on a bed of couscous topped with feta and chopped toasted nuts, if desired.

Mushrooms Lundy

Serves 4: V, V+, GF

The inspiration for this recipe comes from a 1970s vegetarian cookery book called The Vegetarian Epicure by Anna Thomas. Anna's description of her mushroom dish as 'dark and evil' was so intriguing that I just had to try it! Even though the original recipe was delicious, it was too sweet for me. So here is an updated version, which I call Mushrooms Lundy. Serve it over cooked rice or pasta, accompanied by your favourite songs from the 70s.

- 1 Tbsp prepared mustard
- 2 Tbsp Worcestershire sauce
- 2 Tbsp soft brown sugar
- 180ml red wine
- 100ml water
- 1 Tbsp soy sauce
- 1/2 tsp ground black pepper
- 30g butter (or butter substitute)
- 500g mushrooms, sliced 1cm thick
- 1 large onion, chopped
- 1 large red pepper, cut into 1cm squares
- 150g tofu, cut into 1cm squares (If desired)

Combine the mustard, Worcestershire sauce, brown sugar, wine, water, soy sauce and pepper in a small bowl and set aside.

Melt the butter in a large pan over medium heat and add the onion. Cook, stirring occasionally, 3-4 minutes or until the onion has softened. Add the mushrooms and red pepper and cook, stirring, for 4-5 minutes or until the mushrooms have begun to colour.

Pour the reserved sauce over the vegetables and mix well. Simmer gently, uncovered, for 20 minutes, then add tofu, if using. Continue to cook on low heat for another 20 minutes or until the sauce has reduced and is slightly thickened. Serve immediately, over cooked rice or pasta, if desired.

Light Bites

Quesadillas

Serves 4: V, V+

Originally from Mexico, Quesadillas make a fantastic meal or snack at any time of day. Hot, cheesy and filled with lots of tasty extras, they appeal to children and adults alike. Use this recipe as a starting point but don't be limited by it — almost anything goes when it comes to Quesadillas, which are a great way to use up leftovers. And be prepared for plenty of company in the kitchen once you start cooking— these 'little cheesy things' will disappear as quickly as you can make them!

- 200g cheese, grated or finely chopped
- Chopped vegetables: red peppers, sweetcorn, onions, mushrooms, broccoli, butternut squash, sweet potatoes
- Cooked beans: cannellini, chickpeas, red kidney, lentils
- Chopped cooked meats: chorizo, sausage, bacon, ham, chicken
- Chillies, dried herbs and spices, salt and pepper, to taste
- Fresh herbs, if available (coriander and parsley are both good)
- 8 tortilla wraps
- Vegetable oil, for cooking

- Toppings (if desired): guacamole, fresh salsa (made with chopped tomatoes mixed with salt and minced chillies and finished with a squeeze of lime juice)

First, prepare your fillings. Sauté any raw vegetables until tender. Season them with finely chopped fresh chillies (or chilli powder), any herbs/spices you like and salt and pepper, to taste. If you are using fresh coriander or parsley, add plenty of chopped herbs to the vegetables.

To make the quesadillas, heat a frying pan over medium heat. Brush it (or spray it) with a small amount of vegetable oil. Add 1 tortilla to the pan and cover it with 1/4 of the grated cheese. Top the cheese with 1/4 of the cooked vegetables, beans and/or meats. Cover everything with another tortilla and press down lightly. Cook the quesadilla for 2 minutes, then carefully flip the tortilla 'sandwich' over and cook the other side for 2 minutes. The quesadilla is ready to eat when the tortillas have browned and the cheese has melted.

Transfer the quesadilla to a cutting board and cut it into 4 wedges. Repeat with the remaining tortillas. If you are making quesadillas for a crowd, keep them warm in a low oven until you are ready to serve. Eat the quesadillas out of hand or serve them on a warmed plate, topped with guacamole and/or fresh salsa.

Bruschetta

Serves 4: V, V+

Bruschetta make the perfect starter, lunch or snack. These easy, open-face Italian 'sandwiches' are best if you make them just before serving, so that the toasted bread doesn't get soggy. Like Quesadillas, Bruschetta are great for using up any leftovers you've got in the fridge.

- 8 slices of crusty bread such as Tiger or baguette, cut 2cm thick
- 1 garlic clove, cut in half
- Olive oil, to drizzle

Preheat oven to 200 degrees. Arrange the bread in a single layer on a baking tray. Bake for 5 minutes (or until just golden), turning over the slices half-way through baking to ensure even cooking. Remove the bread from the oven and rub each slice with a cut garlic clove. Drizzle lightly with olive oil and set aside until ready to eat. Just before serving, top each slice of bread with a few spoonsful of your chosen topping. Serve immediately.

Classic tomato topping:

- 3 medium tomatoes, chopped
- 2 Tbsp olive oil

- 1 Tbsp pesto
- 2 tsp balsamic vinegar
- Salt and pepper, to taste

Combine all the ingredients in a bowl. Cover and leave at room temperature for at least 30 minutes, for the flavours to develop. Drain the mixture before using it to top the bread slices.

***Beetroot and goats' cheese topping*:**

- 100g goats' cheese
- 2 medium cooked beetroot, finely chopped
- 1 Tbsp balsamic vinegar
- 25g toasted nuts, finely chopped

Combine the beetroot and balsamic in a bowl and mix well. To serve, spread the goats' cheese on the toasted bread and top with the drained beetroot. Sprinkle with the chopped nuts.

Other bruschetta toppings: cooked beans warmed in olive oil, lightly crushed and mixed with chopped fresh herbs; smashed avocado blended with lime juice and topped with toasted sunflower seeds; tinned tuna in oil mixed with chopped olives and a spoonful of tomato puree. Eggs scrambled with cheese is good, too. In fact, just about anything goes!

Mushroom, Leek and Cheese Tartlets

Serves 4: V

This recipe can easily be varied, which makes it ideal for using up any odd bits of cheese and vegetables. Mushroom, Leek and Cheese Tartlets are simple to make but elegant enough to serve to guests. Enjoy them for lunch with a mixed green salad or serve the tartlets as a dinner party starter.

- 1 packet of frozen puff pastry (2 sheets), defrosted
- 50g butter
- 2 large leeks, well washed and thinly sliced
- 100g mushrooms, chopped
- Salt and pepper, to taste
- 4 garlic cloves, finely minced
- 150g Cheddar cheese, grated

Melt the butter in a large saucepan over medium heat. Add the leeks and the mushrooms and salt lightly. Cover and cook gently until the vegetables are just beginning to colour, about 10 minutes. Add the garlic and cook, stirring for 1 minute. Season to taste with salt and pepper. Cool the mixture and then mix in the grated cheese.

Preheat the oven to 180 degrees. Unroll the puff pastry sheets and cut each sheet into 2 evenly sized pieces. Arrange the 4 rectangles of pastry on a baking sheet. Spread the vegetable and cheese mixture evenly onto each pastry rectangle, leaving a 1cm border. Bake for 20 minutes or until pastry is golden and the cheese has melted. Serve immediately.

Variations: *Pizza Tartlets* make a fantastic quick meal. Spread your puff pastry bases with passata or pasta sauce, cover with grated mozzarella and add any pizza toppings you like. Bake at 180 for 30-35 minutes or until the cheese has melted and the pastry is golden.

If you are a fan of Greek food, try this easy version of *Spanakopita Tartlets*: Sauté 1/2 onion in olive oil and add 1/2 bag of fresh spinach (washed and chopped) along with a few teaspoons of water. Cover and cook until the spinach has wilted. Season with salt and pepper to taste, drain and cool. Mix plenty of crumbled feta cheese into the spinach and spoon the mixture onto the puff pastry rectangles. Drizzle the pastries with olive oil and bake at 200 degrees for 10-12 minutes or until the pastry is golden.

Side Dishes

Peperonata

Serves 4: V, V+, GF

This classic Italian dish is wonderfully versatile. Peperonata works equally well as a hot vegetable, a salad or a pasta sauce. Make a big batch and use it to top bruschetta or fill an omelette — it keeps well in the fridge and makes a great veggie sandwich filling, too.

- 4 Tbsp olive oil
- 1 onion, halved and thinly sliced
- 1 clove garlic, finely minced
- 2 red peppers, cored, seeded and cut into 2cm wide strips
- 2 yellow or green peppers, cored, seeded and cut into 2cm wide strips
- 400g tin chopped tomatoes
- Salt and pepper, to taste

Heat the olive oil in a large saucepan over medium heat. Add the onion and garlic and cook, stirring occasionally, until the onion just starts to colour. Add the peppers and tomatoes and stir well to mix. Season to taste with salt and pepper.

Reduce the heat to low, cover and simmer the vegetable mixture for 20 minutes, stirring regularly. Uncover the pan and continue to cook over low heat for another 20 minutes or until the vegetables are very soft and the sauce has thickened, adding a few spoonsful of water if the mixture gets too dry. Serve hot or at room temperature; store any leftovers in the fridge.

Cannellini Mash

Serves 4: V, V+, GF

Cannellini Mash is even easier than mashed potatoes and it makes a nice change, too. Serve it with roast fish, grilled sausages or your favourite vegetable stew.

- 2 Tbsp olive oil
- 4 spring onions, chopped
- 2 garlic cloves, finely minced
- 2x 400g tins cannellini beans, rinsed and drained
- 50ml vegetable stock or water
- Salt and pepper, to taste

Heat the oil in a large saucepan over medium heat. Add the spring onions and garlic and cook, stirring, for 3 minutes or until the vegetables have softened. Add the beans to the pan along with the vegetable stock or water. Cook gently over low heat until the beans are hot.

Using a potato masher, mash the beans roughly. Mix well to blend with the spring onion and garlic. Add plenty of salt and pepper to taste, and serve immediately.

Variations: Try making Mexican-style refried beans. Finely chop an onion and fry it in 2 Tbsp oil until soft. Add a finely chopped garlic clove and fry for one minute. Pour in a tin of kidney or black beans (drained and rinsed) along with a little vegetable stock or water and stir for 3 minutes over medium heat.

Mash the beans until they are almost smooth, then cook gently for another 3 minutes, stirring constantly. Season to taste with salt and pepper.

Refried beans are delicious rolled into tortilla wraps -- top with grated cheese and bake until just heated through. Serve the wraps with guacamole and tomato salsa. Or try refried beans as a side dish for some spicy scrambled eggs.

Patatas Bravas

Serves 4: V, V+, GF

Patatas Bravas are served as tapas in Spain, but they also make a lovely side dish for grilled meat or sausages. I like to serve these piquant potatoes as part of a vegetarian Spanish feast. Patatas Bravas are meant to be spicy hot but you can always reduce the amount of chilli to suit your own taste.

- 500g potatoes, peeled and cut into 2cm cubes
- 4 Tbsp olive oil
- 1 small onion, finely chopped
- 1 garlic clove, finely minced
- 1 fresh chilli, seeded and finely minced or chilli powder, to taste (if desired)
- 400g tin chopped tomatoes
- 1 tsp paprika
- Salt and pepper, to taste
- 2 Tbsp balsamic vinegar

Preheat the oven to 400 degrees. Toss the potatoes with 2 Tbsp of the olive oil and arrange in a single layer on a baking tray. Roast for 45 minutes or until the potatoes are crisp and browned. Salt to taste after roasting.

While the potatoes are cooking, prepare the sauce: heat the remaining 2 Tbsp of olive oil in a saucepan over medium heat and add the onion and garlic. Cook, stirring occasionally, until the onion is golden (5-7 minutes). Add the chilli and cook, stirring constantly, for 1 minute more. Add the tomatoes, paprika and salt and pepper to taste, and stir well. Bring the mixture to the boil, reduce the heat and simmer very gently for 20 minutes or until thickened. Stir in the balsamic vinegar and check for seasoning; add salt and pepper, if needed.

To serve, divide the roast potatoes between serving plates and top with the sauce. Serve immediately.

Cauliflower Fritters

Serves 4: V

Cauliflower Fritters make a fantastic side dish for steak or chops. They can also be enjoyed as a vegetarian main, topped with a chunky tomato sauce or Sweetcorn Salsa. I always grate the cauliflower and the cheese directly into a bowl, which makes for easier clean-up. Don't worry if you end up with some larger pieces of cauli— they'll add a nice texture to the cooked fritters.

- 1/2 medium cauliflower, grated
- 70g Cheddar cheese, grated
- 1/2 onion, finely chopped
- 1 egg
- 3 Tbsp corn flour
- Salt and pepper, to taste
- 1-2 Tbsp vegetable oil, for frying

Put all of the ingredients except the vegetable oil into a large bowl and mix well.

Heat 1 Tbsp of oil in a frying pan on medium heat. Add a couple of spoonsful of cauliflower mixture to the pan and shape the mound quickly into a patty. You should be able to fit 4 patties into the pan at once.

Cook the fritters on one side until they are brown and crispy (about 5 minutes), then flip them over and cook for another 5 minutes. Resist the urge to flip the fritters until they are thoroughly cooked on the first side or they will fall apart.

Keep the first batch of cooked fritters warm in a 100 degree oven while you fry the remainder of the mixture (add more oil to the pan if needed). As soon as all of the mixture has been cooked, serve the fritters immediately.

Greek-style Spinach

Serves 4: V, V+, GF

Horta is the Greek name for this traditional spring treat. All over Greece, families go out into the countryside and forage for wild greens to use in this much-loved dish. On Lundy, fresh spinach from the Shop makes a fine substitute for wild greens.

- 4 Tbsp olive oil (extra virgin, if possible)
- 4 spring onions, chopped
- 1 garlic clove, finely minced
- 500g fresh spinach, washed
- 50ml water
- Juice of 1/2 lemon
- Salt and pepper, to taste

Heat 2 Tbsp of the olive oil in a large pan over medium-high heat. Add the spring onions and garlic and cook, stirring constantly, for 1 minute. Add the spinach to the pan along with the water and cook, stirring occasionally, until the spinach has wilted, 5-7 minutes.

Season the spinach to taste with salt and pepper and drizzle with the remaining 2 Tbsp of olive oil and the lemon juice. Mix well and serve.

Variation: To turn this dish into a hearty vegetarian main, add a large handful of rice to the hot oil along with the onions and garlic. Stir fry for a minute or two until the grains become opaque. Increase the amount of water to 250ml, add the spinach and water to the pan and bring to the boil. If you've got some dill weed (fresh or dried), add a bit to the spinach and rice mixture – it makes a nice addition.

Cover and cook (stirring occasionally) for 20 minutes or until the rice is tender and the water has been absorbed. Finish the dish with olive oil and lemon juice, and serve with crusty bread.

Baking

To make the recipes in this chapter, you will need to measure your ingredients using the Tala Cook's Measure or the Pyrex Kitchen Lab found in every Lundy kitchen. Precision is important in baking, so when measuring dry ingredients in the jug be sure to level their tops to ensure accuracy.

Apple Crumb Tart

Serves 4-6: V

Apple puddings are always popular and this one couldn't be easier. If you've got berries or chopped nuts to use up, go ahead and add them to the pudding mixture — they'll make great additions. Some mixed spice is also nice, especially in the colder weather.

- 200g digestive biscuits, crushed into fine crumbs (see Note below)
- 60g caster sugar
- 50g butter, softened
- 4 apples, peeled, cored and thinly sliced
- 70g soft dark brown sugar
- 15g butter, divided (for crumb topping)
- Pouring cream or ice cream to serve, if desired

Preheat the oven to 180 degrees. Put the digestive biscuit crumbs, caster sugar and softened butter into a medium sized bowl. Using a fork, blend the mixture until thoroughly mixed. Pour just over half of the crumb mixture into a Pyrex pie dish and spread evenly, pressing the mixture firmly into the dish.

Arrange the sliced apples over the crumb crust and sprinkle evenly with the brown sugar. Top with the remaining crumb mix and dot everything with the 15g butter. Bake for 45 minutes or until the apples are tender and the topping has browned. Serve hot, with pouring cream or ice cream, if desired.

Note: The best way to crush digestive biscuits is between 2 sheets of kitchen roll. Do not detach the sheets from one another, just place them on the worktop. Roughly break the biscuits into bits, lay them on the bottom sheet and fold the top sheet over them. Then roll over the biscuits (gently!) with a rolling pin until they turn into fine crumbs. Lift the kitchen roll carefully and pour the crumbs into a mixing bowl.

Lemon Sponge Pudding

Serves 4-6: V

This fabulous retro pudding is always a hit with family and friends. As if by magic, the batter separates during baking into a sponge layer and a tangy lemon sauce. Served hot, Lemon Sponge Pudding makes the perfect finale to a special meal.

- 75g butter, softened (plus extra, to grease)
- 200g caster sugar
- Finely grated zest and juice of 3 lemons
- 3 eggs, separated
- 75g self-raising flour
- 200ml milk
- Whipped cream for serving, if desired

Preheat the oven to 180 degrees and grease a 1.5l baking dish. In a large bowl, cream together the butter, sugar and lemon zest until fluffy and light. Beat in the egg yolks, one at a time, until well blended. Stir in the flour, then gradually add the milk and lemon juice. Don't worry if the mixture looks curdled at this point - it will be fine.

In a separate clean bowl, whisk the egg whites until they have reached the soft peak stage. Fold them gently into the lemon batter and pour the mixture into the greased baking dish. Bake for about 40 minutes or until the sponge top is golden and firm.

Serve immediately, scooping down to the bottom of the dish so that each serving gets a portion of sponge as well as sauce. Top with whipped cream, if desired.

Caribbean Carrot Pudding

Serves 4-6: V

Loosely based on the classic Indian sweet, carrot halwa, this easy baked pudding will remind you of carrot cake. Caribbean Carrot Pudding's combination of rum, raisins and spices make it the perfect dessert for a festive winter meal. Start soaking the raisins at least an hour before you begin to mix the pudding, so that they've got plenty of time to absorb the rum.

- 1 mug full of raisins
- 120ml dark rum
- 120g butter, softened
- 125g sugar
- 4 medium carrots, finely grated
- 75g plain flour
- 1/2 tsp salt
- 2 tsp baking powder
- 1 tsp mixed spice
- 2 eggs, beaten
- Whipped or pouring cream, to serve

Put the raisins into a bowl, pour over the rum and soak for at least 1 hour.

Prepare a 1 litre soufflé dish by buttering it well. Preheat the oven to 180 degrees. Cream the butter with the sugar, mixing until light. Add the carrots along with the raisins and any remaining rum, and mix well. Stir in the flour, salt, baking powder and mixed spice, continuing to mix until the batter is well blended. Fold in the beaten eggs and stir very gently until the eggs have been mixed in.

Pour the mixture into the prepared dish and bake for 40 minutes or until the pudding is completely cooked (it will feel firm when lightly pressed). Serve warm with whipped or pouring cream.

Irish Potato Farls

Serves 4: V

Potato Farls couldn't be easier to make and they are wonderfully versatile — think of them as flatbreads that work as well with a cooked breakfast as they do with a curry. They are also a great way to use up leftover mashed potato — just add enough flour for the mixture to hold together and prepare as in the recipe below. Serve Potato Farls for breakfast with butter and salt (or jam) or enjoy them as a simple supper, topped with crisp bacon and melted cheese or a ladle of your favourite vegetable stew.

- 500g potatoes, peeled and cut into quarters
- 50g butter
- 60g plain flour, plus extra for rolling out
- Large pinch of baking powder
- Salt and black pepper
- Milk (if needed)
- Extra butter, for frying

Put the potatoes into a large saucepan, cover with water, add a large pinch of salt and bring to the boil. Reduce the heat, cover and cook for 15 minutes or until the potatoes are quite tender. Drain them well and return them to the pan.

In a small saucepan, melt the 50g butter. Pour the melted butter into the potatoes and mash them well, using a potato masher. Stir in the flour, baking powder and salt and pepper to taste, mixing well until the dough comes together and pulls away from the sides of the pan. If it is too dry, add a little milk. If it is too wet, add a bit more flour.

Divide the dough into two halves. Flour a surface and roll the first half of the dough into a 15cm diameter circle. The circle should be no more than 1cm thick. Cut the dough into quarters to form the farls.

Melt a knob of butter in a frying pan over medium heat and carefully add the farls to the pan. Cook for 3 minutes or until golden brown, then flip the farls and cook their other sides for another 3 minutes. Remove the cooked farls and keep them warm while cooking the remaining dough (as above). Serve immediately, with toppings of your choice.

Desserts

Roast Grapes with Yoghurt and Honey

Serves 4: V, GF

This simple recipe is inspired by a gorgeous pudding I had at a seaside taverna in Crete. Roasting the grapes enhances their sweetness and flavour and also produces a lovely rich juice. Roast grapes are perfect as a pudding, but they also make a fantastic accompaniment to roast pork or duck. Or use the grapes to top a salad made with beetroot, celery, goats' cheese and chopped nuts.

- 400g seedless grapes, removed from their stems
- 1 Tbsp olive oil
- 450g Greek style yoghurt
- 4 Tbsp runny honey

Preheat the oven to 180 degrees. Toss the grapes with the olive oil and spread them out in a single layer on a baking tray. Roast for 35-45 minutes or until the grapes have collapsed and started to produce juice.

To serve this pudding warm, divide the grapes and their juices between 4 bowls, top with the yoghurt and drizzle with the honey.

If you are planning to serve the grapes later, remove them to a bowl along with their juice. Cover and store in the fridge until ready to use.

Note: Roasted grapes are also delicious served over a plain cake or a scoop of vanilla ice cream.

Jamaican Banana Sauté

Serves 4: V, GF

This Caribbean pudding takes only minutes to prepare and is absolutely delicious. Topped with pouring cream or vanilla ice cream, Jamaican Banana Sauté makes an elegant dessert for a dinner party. Garnish with chopped nuts for an extra treat.

- 4 ripe bananas, peeled and sliced lengthwise into quarters
- 30g butter
- 2 Tbsp soft dark brown sugar
- Juice of 1 lemon
- Pinch of salt
- 60ml dark rum

Melt the butter in a frying pan over medium heat and add the bananas. Sauté, turning occasionally, until they have softened, 5-7 minutes. Add the brown sugar, lemon juice and salt and mix gently but thoroughly (try not to break the bananas).

Pour in the rum and continue to cook until the rum is heated through. Serve immediately, with the juices poured over.

Chocolate Caramel Sauce

Serves 4-6: V, GF

This ultra-rich dessert sauce will turn any boring pudding into a special occasion treat. Spoon Chocolate Caramel Sauce over ice cream or plain cake, or use it as a dipping sauce for fresh fruits such as strawberries or pear slices. If you're lucky enough to end up with leftover sauce, chill it to make a fantastic spread for toast or croissants.

- 120g dark chocolate
- 175g soft dark brown sugar
- 120ml double cream
- 15g butter

Melt the chocolate in a medium saucepan over low heat, stirring regularly. Add the sugar, cream and butter and cook, continuing to stir, until the sauce has thickened. Cool slightly before serving. Store any leftovers in the fridge.

Mixed Berry Slump

Serves 6: V

Slumps (also known as grunts) are old-fashioned American fruit puddings that are cooked on the hob rather than in the oven. In this recipe, mixed berries are paired with tender steamed dumplings and served warm with cream (or ice cream). Even though Mixed Berry Slump is supposed to serve 6 people, don't be surprised if everyone asks for seconds!

- 3 mugs full of frozen summer fruits
- 120g sugar, plus 2 Tbsp for dumplings
- 300ml water
- Grated zest and juice of 1/2 lemon
- 125g plain flour
- 2 tsp baking powder
- 1/2 tsp salt
- 15g butter
- 120ml milk
- Cream or ice cream, to serve

In a large saucepan, combine the berries, the 120g sugar, water, lemon zest and juice and bring to the boil. Reduce the heat and simmer, uncovered, for 5 minutes.

While the berries are cooking, combine the flour, the 2 Tbsp sugar, baking powder and salt in a large bowl. Rub in the butter until the mixture resembles coarse crumbs. Add the milk quickly and stir until the mixture is just blended. It will be a soft dough.

Drop the dough by the spoonful onto the berries, making 6 dumplings. Cover the pan tightly and cook over low heat for 10 minutes. Do not lift the lid while the dumplings are cooking or they will not rise.

To serve, spoon the dumplings into serving bowls and top with the cooked berries. Serve warm with cream or ice cream, if desired.

Ice Cream with Mix-ins

Serves 4: V, V+, GF

Turn plain vanilla ice cream into a fun DIY treat with this easy recipe. The more mix-ins you offer, the better — people love to come up with their own flavour combinations. If you're vegan, you can enjoy this pudding with non-dairy ice cream and vegan mix-ins. Have fun — the sky's the limit!

- 500ml vanilla ice cream
- Mix-ins: chopped chocolate bars, crumbled biscuits or cake, chopped dried fruit, chopped nuts, fresh or tinned fruit (berries, peach or pineapple chunks, etc.), breakfast cereal (muesli, Coco Pops, Country Crisp, etc.), peanut butter, Nutella, jam, honey, assorted liqueurs

Soften the ice cream by putting it in the fridge for 20-30 minutes before eating. While the ice cream is softening prepare a selection of mix-ins, putting each one into a separate bowl or jug.

To serve, divide the softened ice cream amongst 4 bowls. Encourage your guests to add as many mix-ins as they'd like. Ice cream with mix-ins is best when it is well stirred before eating, so that the mix-ins are evenly distributed. Enjoy!

More Salmagundi

As an honoured guest at a 17th century dinner, you might have enjoyed a Salmagundi. These large salads were known for their inventive use of ingredients – one early recipe mixed cooked chicken with raw oysters, figs, peas, potatoes, oranges and almonds! Although that particular combination of flavours may not appeal to modern tastes, the concept is still a good one. That's why I've written **More Salmagundi** *– to inspire you to use leftover ingredients in creative and interesting ways.*

So if you find yourself with a few spring onions or a spoonful of pesto, please don't bin them. Instead have a look at the alphabetical list of ingredients in **More Salmagundi**, *where you will find lots of delicious recipes and tips to help you to reduce your food waste.*

Apples

Recipes:

Apple Crumb Tart

Apple Brown Betty

Grilled Cheese and Tomato Sandwiches

Suggestions:

- For a quick and easy pudding, make **Baked Stuffed Apples:** core 4 apples, cut a very thin slice off the bottom of each one (so they sit upright) and place them in a roasting tin. In a small bowl, blend 3 Tbsp brown sugar with 2 Tbsp raisins and 3 Tbsp chopped nuts. Stuff the filling equally into the apples and top with a small knob of butter. Pour 100ml of water or apple juice into the tin and bake in a 180 degree oven for 45 minutes or until the apples are tender. Serve hot with the cooking juices spooned over, accompanied by pouring cream or custard, if desired. **V, V+, GF**

- Make **Apple and Mars Bar Sandwiches** (an Ulster recipe which has become a firm favourite at our house!): slice the apples and Mars bars very thinly. Butter slices of bread (white or brown) and arrange a single layer of apple slices on each slice of bread. Top with slices of Mars bar and cover with another slice of buttered bread. Cut each sandwich into halves or fingers and enjoy!

Apricot Jam

Recipes:

Apricot Barbecue Chicken

Suggestions:

- Make **Apricot Sauce**: melt jam over low heat, along with a few spoonsful of water (or rum). Serve warm, spooned over cheesecake or ice cream. **V, V+**

- Add a small pot of apricot jam to your **Cheese Platter.** Delicious spooned over goats' cheese, blue cheese or brie. **V**

- Make an **Apricot Filled Cake**: slice any plain cake horizontally and spread a thick layer of apricot jam on the bottom half. Sprinkle the jam with chopped chocolate and nuts (if desired) and cover with the top half of the cake. Cut carefully into slices and serve with whipped or pouring cream, if desired. **V**

Bread

Recipes:

The Best Macaroni and Cheese

Bruschetta

Pitta Bread Pizza

Grilled Cheese and Tomato Sandwiches

Suggestions:

- Make **Apple Brown Betty**: butter a baking dish and arrange alternating layers of chopped apples and stale breadcrumbs (start and end with a breadcrumb layer). Sprinkle a pinch of mixed spice and a generous amount sugar onto each layer of apples. Bake until golden brown and serve with pouring cream, if desired. **V**

- Make **Cheese-topped Croutons**: these are best made with baguette or a Tiger loaf but any bread will do. Slice the bread 1cm thick, drizzle it with olive oil and toast it briefly under a hot grill (keep an eye on it as it can burn quickly).

Grate enough cheese (dairy or vegan) to cover the tops of your bread, cover the slices evenly with cheese and grill until melted. Serve your croutons immediately on top of hot soup or use them to accompany salads or stews. **V, V+**

Butter

Recipes:

Baked Corn Custard

Irish Potato Farls

Garlic Butter

Jamaican Banana Sauté

Caribbean Carrot Pudding

Apple Crumb Tart

Chocolate Caramel Sauce

Suggestions:

- Make **Brown Butter Sauce**: a classic sauce which couldn't be easier to make. Melt a quantity of butter in a small saucepan over medium heat, stirring occasionally, for 4-6 minutes or until the butter is nutty and brown. Remove from the heat and serve immediately as a sauce for fish or pasta. If desired, garlic or herbs can be added to the butter as it browns, for extra flavour. **V, GF**

- Make **Blue Cheese Butter**: soften the butter and crumble an equal amount of blue cheese into it. Blend with a fork until it is quite smooth (some lumps are fine). Put the mixture into the fridge for a couple of hours (or more), to allow the flavours to blend. Use Blue Cheese Butter as a topping for freshly cooked vegetables, mix it into mashed potatoes or melt it over a grilled steak. **V**

Cabbage

Recipes:

North African Vegetable Stew

Suggestions:

- Make a classic **Coleslaw**: core and finely shred 1/4 cabbage. Add 1 grated carrot and 2 thinly sliced green onions. For the dressing, whisk together 4 Tbsp mayonnaise, 2 tsp vinegar, 1/2 tsp mustard and salt and pepper, to taste. Pour over the cabbage mixture, mix well and serve. Store any leftovers in the fridge. **V, GF**

- Make **Creamed Cabbage:** finely shred half a cabbage. In a large saucepan, melt a knob of butter and sauté half an onion (finely chopped) along with 1 garlic clove (finely minced) for 5 minutes. Add a 2cm length of fresh ginger, peeled and grated (if desired) and cook for another minute. Add the shredded cabbage and cook, stirring occasionally, for 15-20 minutes or until tender. Pour in 100ml double cream and reduce heat. Cover and simmer for 10 minutes. Season to taste with salt and pepper. Serve immediately. **V, GF**

Celery

Recipes:

Cajun Fish Soup

Fattoush

Sweet Potato Salad

Chinese Beef Stew

Suggestions:

- Make **Stuffed Celery Sticks**: cut celery into 6cm lengths and fill the centres with blue cheese or Boursin. **V, GF**

- Make **Braised Celery**: slice celery into 2cm lengths. In a large saucepan, melt a knob of butter. Add finely chopped onion and sauté over medium heat until soft. Add the celery to pan, stir to coat with butter and pour over enough vegetable stock to come half-way up celery. Reduce heat, cover and simmer for 10-15 minutes or until celery is tender. Season to taste. Braised celery makes a good accompaniment to roast fish or chicken, or serve it as a veggie main over cooked rice. **V, GF**

- Add celery sticks to a **Crudités Platter** that includes carrot sticks, green or red peppers (cut into thin slices) and raw cauliflower florets. Serve with **Olive Dip** or ready-made hummus or tzatziki for an easy starter or snack. **V, V+, GF**

Cheese

Recipes:

Feta-topped Mediterranean Fish Fillets

Cheese-stuffed Pork Chops

The Best Macaroni and Cheese

Pasta Almost Carbonara

Pasta with Aubergine and Mozzarella

Quesadillas

Bruschetta Blue Cheese Butter

Mushroom, Leek and Cheese Tartlets

Cheese-topped Croutons

Grilled Cheese and Tomato Sandwiches

Suggestions:

- Make **Cheesy Mashed Potatoes**: mix a handful of grated cheese into homemade mashed potatoes for added richness and flavour. Cheddar and blue cheese are especially good. **V, GF**

- Make Greek **Feta and Yoghurt Sauce**: blend 2 parts Greek yoghurt with 1 part crumbled feta cheese. Add chopped fresh mint (if available) and a splash of lemon juice. Serve as a dip with pitta chips or crudités, or use to top lamb burgers. **V, GF**

- Make **Pitta Bread Pizza**: Anything goes when it comes to these easy pizzas. Place pitta breads on a baking tray. Cover with passata (or any other sauce you'd like), then add your choice of toppings: shredded cooked chicken, sausage or bacon bits, sautéed mushrooms, roast vegetables, etc. Finish with your favourite grated or crumbled cheese and bake at 200 degrees for 10 minutes or until the cheese has melted. **V**

Chutney

Recipes:

Cheese-stuffed Pork Chops

Lamb and Sweet Potato Stew

Suggestions:

- Make **Chutney Glazed Chicken**: mix chutney with a few spoonsful of fruit juice (or water) to thin to glaze consistency. Spread over chicken portions before roasting, basting occasionally while cooking. **GF**

- Make **Chutney Dressing** by blending chutney with mayonnaise and/or Greek yoghurt. This dressing is especially good in a salad made from cubed cooked chicken, celery and apples or grapes. Serve the salad on a bed of lettuce or as a sandwich filling. **V, GF**

Coconut Milk

Recipes:

Spicy Coconut Cucumbers

Suggestions:

- Make **Coconut Rice**: substitute coconut milk for half of the water when cooking rice. Coconut rice is the perfect accompaniment to any curry or Thai dish. **V, V+, GF**

- Stir a couple of spoonsful of coconut milk into a **Vegetable Stir Fry** made with onion, garlic, fresh chilli, thinly sliced carrots, celery and shredded butternut squash. Serve over white or brown rice for an easy vegan main. **V, V+, GF**

Eggs

Recipes:

Lundy Miso Soup

Cobb Salad

The Best Macaroni and Cheese

Cauliflower Fritters

Caribbean Carrot Pudding

Suggestions:

- Make a quick **Nicoise-style Salad**: on a bed of salad greens arrange tomatoes (quartered), sliced cucumber, sliced green onions, slices of cooked potato and olives (if desired). Top with tinned tuna (well drained and flaked) and hard-boiled eggs (quartered). Drizzle with vinaigrette dressing and serve immediately, with additional dressing on the side. **V, GF**

- Make a Greek **Avgolemono (Egg and Lemon) Soup**: in a large saucepan, bring 1 litre of chicken stock to the boil. Add a handful of rice, cover and simmer for 20 minutes. As soon as the rice is tender, whisk 2 eggs together with the juice of 1 large lemon. Ladle about 150ml of the hot broth into the egg/lemon mixture and whisk to combine. Stir the egg mixture into the simmering soup and cook for 1-2 minutes, or until the soup is thickened. Season to taste with salt and pepper and serve immediately. **GF**

- **Asparagus with Eggs** is a classic combination. Cook fresh asparagus until just tender, drizzle with a lemony vinaigrette dressing and top with finely chopped hard-boiled egg. This dish makes an elegant starter or a lovely light lunch during asparagus season. **V, GF**

Garlic

Suggestions:

- Make **Spaghetti Aglio e Olio:** For 4 people, cook 400g spaghetti in boiling water until al dente. Drain the pasta and set it aside, reserving 500ml of the cooking water. In a frying pan, heat 4 Tbsp of olive oil and sauté 6 thinly sliced garlic cloves for 2-3 minutes or until golden brown. Add the pasta cooking water to the frying pan and bring the mixture to the boil. Reduce heat and simmer for 5 minutes or until liquid is reduced by half. Add the cooked pasta to the pan and toss for 1-2 minutes over low heat, so that the sauce completely coats the spaghetti. Serve immediately, topped with grated Grana Padano cheese. So simple and delicious! **V**

- Make **Garlic Butter:** soften 100g butter and mix in 1-2 garlic cloves, crushed and then very finely minced. Add some finely minced parsley, if available. Put the garlic butter in the fridge for a couple of hours for the flavours to blend. Use the butter to make garlic bread or melt it as a sauce for fish, seafood, steaks or vegetables. **V, GF**

Ginger

Recipes:

Lundy Miso Soup

Chinese Beef Stew

Soy Glazed Chicken with Roast Broccoli

Creamed Cabbage

Soy Salad Dressing

Suggestions:

- Make **Ginger Roast Salmon**: in a small bowl, mix 3 Tbsp finely minced ginger with 1 Tbsp olive oil, 1 Tbsp lime juice and 1 tsp honey. Season to taste with salt and pepper. Spread the ginger mixture onto four salmon fillets before roasting them in a hot oven. Serve with white rice and stir-fried vegetables, if desired. **GF**

- Make a **Fruit Sauce**: chop apples or pears and put them in a saucepan with some water. Add sugar to taste and some finely minced ginger. Cover and simmer until soft. Serve with roast pork or as a dessert sauce over ice cream.

- Make a simple **Asian-style Chicken Soup**. Start by sautéing finely minced garlic and ginger in hot oil along with a pinch of turmeric (if desired). Add hot chicken stock to the saucepan and bring to the boil. Stir in some dried egg noodles and cook for 3 minutes. Add diced chicken, a few shredded spinach leaves (if desired) and a squeeze of lemon juice. Serve immediately, topped with sliced spring onion.

Honey

Recipes:

Soy Glazed Chicken with Roast Broccoli

Spicy Coconut Cucumbers

Quesadillas

Ginger Roast Salmon

Suggestions:

- Make **Honey Salad Dressing:** whisk 1 Tbsp honey with 2 tsp grainy mustard, 6 Tbsp olive oil and the juice of one lemon. Add salt and pepper to taste. This dressing is especially good on any salad that includes fruit. **V, GF**

- Make **Honey Roast Carrots:** slice 6 carrots lengthwise and then across into 6cm lengths. Whisk 2 Tbsp honey together with 1 Tbsp olive oil, add salt and pepper to taste. Toss carrots in honey/oil mixture and spread them in a single layer on a baking tray. Roast at 200 degrees for 35-45 minutes or until tender and slightly browned. Serve hot. **V, GF**

Mustard

Recipes:

Carrot Salad with Lemon Mustard Dressing

Sweet Potato Salad

Cobb Salad

Honey Salad Dressing

Steak and Spinach with Mustard Sauce

Braised Chicken with Leeks and Peas

Mushrooms Lundy

Suggestions:

- Make **Grilled Cheese and Tomato Sandwiches**: spread a slice of bread with grainy mustard and sprinkle evenly with shredded Cheddar cheese. Top the cheese with thin tomato slices and then cover the tomato with more grated cheese. Cover the sandwich with another slice of bread and butter the top of the bread generously. Heat a frying pan (over medium heat) and fry the sandwich butter side down for 2 minutes, pressing it firmly with a fish slice. Butter the top of the sandwich generously, flip it over and continue cooking for another 2 minutes or until the cheese is melted and the bread is toasted. Cool slightly, cut the sandwich in half and serve. **V**

- Make **Mustard Mash**: mix either 1 tsp English mustard (or to taste) or 2-3 Tbsp grainy mustard into mashed potatoes to serve 4. Mustard Mash goes especially well with grilled sausages or roast salmon; it is also nice topped with a bean stew. **V, V+, GF**

Olive oil

Recipes:

Many of the recipes in *More Lundy Cookery* call for small amounts of olive oil. For recipes that use 50ml or more, check out the **Salads** chapter.

Pasta with Fresh Broccoli

Roast Fish with White Beans and Olives

Suggestions:

- Make **Vegan Mashed Potatoes**: boil 700g potatoes, peeled and cubed, in salted water until soft. Add 2 Tbsp extra virgin olive oil and 120ml milk substitute and mash until smooth. Season to taste with plenty of salt and pepper. Serves 4. **V, V+, GF**

- Make **Vegan Garlic Bread:** slice a baguette lengthwise. Mix extra virgin olive oil with very finely chopped garlic, to taste (add chopped parsley, if desired) and spread the mixture on the bread. Bake at 200 degrees for 5-7 minutes or until crisp and golden. Serve hot. **V, V+**

Olives

Recipes:

Fattoush

Picadillo

Roast Fish with White Beans and Olives

Spanish Rice

Suggestions:

- Make **Pasta with Olives**: heat 2 Tbsp olive oil over medium heat and sauté 2 garlic cloves, minced, until soft. Add a handful of chopped olives and a 400g tin of chopped tomatoes. Simmer, covered, for 10 minutes. Mix sauce with cooked pasta and top with grated Grana Padano cheese, if desired. **V, V+**

- Make a classic American **Olive Dip**: mix together 2 parts softened Philadelphia Soft Cheese with 1 part mayonnaise. Stir in lots of finely chopped green olives. Chill for 1 hour or more before serving, to blend flavours. Serve with crackers, crisps or crudités. **V, GF**

Peas (frozen)

Recipes:

Braised Chicken with Leeks and Peas

Italian Chicken with Lemon and Wine

Lamb and Sweet Potato Stew

Pasta Almost Carbonara

Suggestions:

- Make a **Creamy Pea Salad**: cook 2 mugs full of peas until just tender. Fry 4 rashers of streaky bacon until crisp, drain and chop into small bits. For the dressing, whisk together 2 Tbsp of mayonnaise with 2 Tbsp of Greek yoghurt. Add 1 tsp vinegar and salt and pepper to taste. Mix the dressing into the peas and stir in the bacon bits. Cool and chill until serving. **GF**

- Make a **Quick Pasta Sauce** by mixing cooked peas and a tin of tuna (drained and flaked) with a tub of ready-made tzatziki. Stir gently into cooked pasta and serve hot, or chill and serve cold as a pasta salad.

- Make **Pea Risotto**: Start by sautéing half a finely chopped onion in 2 Tbsp olive oil. Add a mug full of Arborio rice and stir for 1 minute. Add a glass of white wine and cook for another 2-3 minutes. Gradually add hot vegetable stock to the rice, stirring constantly until the liquid is absorbed before adding the next ladleful of stock (you will need about 700ml of stock altogether). When the rice is soft and most of the liquid is gone, add a mug full of peas along with a handful of grated Grana Padano cheese. Heat, stirring, until the peas are warm and the cheese has melted. Season to taste with salt and pepper and serve immediately.
  V, GF

Pesto

Recipes:

Bean and Pesto Soup

Fattoush

Bruschetta

Suggestions:

- Make **Pesto and Goats' Cheese Pinwheels**: mix 1 part goats' cheese with 1 part soft cheese. Spread cheese mixture onto a tortilla wrap and top with pesto, spreading the pesto evenly over the cheese. Roll the wrap tightly and chill it until ready to serve. Cut the roll into 2cm slices and serve as a canapé with drinks. **V**

- Make **Pesto-roasted Chicken Breasts or Salmon** by spreading pesto evenly on the chicken or fish fillets and roasting in a 200 degree oven for 25 minutes or until thoroughly cooked.

- For an easy **Tomato Pesto Pasta Sauce**, mix a couple of spoonsful of pesto into a jar of passata and heat until piping hot. **V, V+, GF**

Soy Sauce

Recipes:

Lundy Miso Soup

Soy Glazed Chicken with Roast Broccoli

Chinese Beef Stew

Mushrooms Lundy

Suggestions:

- Make an **East Asian Style Salad Dressing**: whisk together 2 Tbsp of each of the following: soy sauce, balsamic vinegar and vegetable oil. Stir in some grated fresh ginger and finely chopped spring onions. This dressing is especially good with a salad made from finely shredded cabbage mixed with thinly sliced radishes and cucumbers. Mix in some cold cooked noodles for a quick summer lunch. **V, V+**

- Add loads of extra flavour to green vegetables such as spinach, kale and broccoli by **stir frying** them with garlic and a splash of soy sauce. **V, V+**

Spring onions

Recipes:

Lundy Miso Soup

Carrot Salad with Lemon Mustard Dressing

Fattoush

Cobb Salad

Steak and Spinach with Mustard Sauce

Greek-Style Spinach

Cannellini Mash

Spicy Coconut Cucumbers

Spaghetti Almost Carbonara

The Best Macaroni and Cheese

Seared Tuna with Pineapple Salsa

Suggestions:

- **Roast spring onions** alongside fish fillets (and fresh asparagus, if available) for a wonderful spring meal. Simple toss the vegetables in olive oil and sprinkle with salt before adding to the roasting tin next to the fish. Roast at 180 degrees for 25 minutes or until the fish flakes easily and the vegetables are tender. **GF**

- **Liven up a sandwich** by adding finely chopped spring onions to egg mayonnaise or to shredded Cheddar cheese mixed with a bit of mayo. **V**

Sweet Chilli Sauce

Recipes:

Lundy Miso Soup

Suggestions:

- Make **Spicy Cheese Dip**: mix chilli sauce (to taste) into softened Philadelphia Soft Cheese and serve with tortilla chips or crudités. **V, GF**

- Use sweet chilli sauce as a **tasty glaze** for sausages, chicken portions or salmon fillets — simply brush over the meat or fish towards the end of the cooking time. **GF**

- Mix a spoonful of chilli sauce into any **stir-fried vegetables** for extra flavour and zing. **V, V+, GF**

Sweetcorn

Recipes:

Corn Chowder

Cajun Fish Soup

Cobb Salad

Three Sisters Stew

Baked Corn Custard

Quesadillas

Bruschetta

Suggestions:

- Make **Sweetcorn Salsa**: mix sweetcorn with chopped tomato and spring onions. Add finely chopped fresh chilli and salt and pepper, to taste. Dress the mixture with olive oil and a squeeze of fresh lime juice. Serve with Cauliflower Fritters, roasted fish fillets or any Mexican-style dish. **V, V+, GF**

- Make **Creamy Sweetcorn Pasta**: sauté finely minced onion in butter until soft. Add sweetcorn and cook, stirring, until golden. Pour in double cream mixed with an equal amount of vegetable stock, then add a handful of grated Grana Padano cheese. Cook, stirring constantly, until the cheese has melted and the sauce has thickened (about 5 minutes). Season to taste with salt and pepper. Stir the sauce into cooked pasta and serve immediately with more grated cheese, if desired. **V**

Tomato puree

Recipes:

Bean and Pesto Soup

Portuguese Pork Chops

Spanish Rice

Suggestions:

- Make **Homemade Ketchup**: blend 100g tomato puree with 30ml balsamic vinegar (or to taste). Now get creative — season your ketchup with salt, pepper, ground chillies, mixed spice or any combination of herbs and spices you prefer. Store in the fridge. **V, V+, GF**

- Add an **umami hit** to your cooking by squeezing a spoonful of tomato puree into onions when you are sautéing them. A spoonful of tomato puree will also enhance your stews and meat braises. You won't taste the tomato, but you will notice the extra-savoury goodness. **V, V+, GF**

Vinegar

Recipes:

Sweet Potato Salad

Cobb Salad

Portuguese Pork Chops

Bruschetta

Patatas Bravas

Homemade Ketchup

Suggestions:

- Make **Strawberries with Balsamic Vinegar**: in this unexpected combination, the balsamic enhances the flavour of the strawberries. To prepare, slice a punnet of strawberries, sprinkle them with 1 1/2 Tbsp balsamic vinegar and 3 Tbsp sugar and toss gently so the berries are well coated. Leave for half an hour at room temperature so that the flavours have time to blend. Serve over cheesecake, a plain sponge or ice cream. Store any leftovers in the fridge. **V, V+, GF**

- Blend balsamic vinegar with salt and honey (to taste) and mix with chopped cooked beetroot for a quick and **easy 'pickle'**. Store any leftovers in the fridge. **V, GF**

Worcestershire Sauce

Recipes:

Portuguese Pork Chops

Mushrooms Lundy

Steak and Spinach with Mustard Sauce

Suggestions:

- Make an easy **Cheese Sauce**: Put 500ml milk, 50g butter and 4 Tbsp flour into a large saucepan over high heat. Whisk constantly — the butter will melt and the mixture will come to the boil and begin to thicken. Continue to cook, whisking constantly, for another 2 minutes. Reduce the heat to low and stir in 1 tsp Worcestershire sauce and 120g grated Cheddar cheese. Remove from heat and use immediately for cauliflower cheese, mac and cheese or as a sauce for fish or cooked vegetables.

- **Mix Worcestershire sauce into eggs** before scrambling (1/4 tsp for 2 eggs) for extra flavour.

Acknowledgements

Many thanks to Sue Waterfield, the manager of Lundy General Stores, for her support as well as her expertise. I could not have written *More Lundy Cookery* without her.

Special thanks to all of the islanders and visitors who took the time to tell me what they'd like to see in this book. I hope they will enjoy cooking from it as much as I enjoyed writing it.

Finally, my love and appreciation to my amazing husband, who encouraged me in late 2009 to write a book about cooking on Lundy. Who could have imagined that more than a decade later, I would be doing it again?!

About the Author

Ilene Sterns is the author of the original *Lundy Cookery*. She is an artist/photographer as well as a keen cook. Ilene lives in a North Wiltshire village with her husband, Phil Atkin.

www.ingramcontent.com/pod-product-compliance
Lightning Source LLC
LaVergne TN
LVHW051607070426
835507LV00021B/2809